THE SECRET CURRENCY

LEVERAGING YOUR BUSINESS WITH BARTER

VERNE GARDINER

40°

© 2012 Verne Gardiner

ISBN: 9780987243119 (e-book)

NATIONAL LIBRARY OF AUSTRALIA CATALOGUING-IN-PUBLICATION ENTRY
Author: Gardiner, Verne.
Title: Leveraging your business with barter: the secret currency /
  Verne Gardiner.
ISBN: 9780987124456 (pbk.)
Subjects:
  Barter.
  Success in business.
  Economics.
  Wealth.
Dewey Number: 332.54

Published by Forty Degrees South Pty Ltd
Hobart Tasmania, Australia
www.fortysouth.com.au

Design and production by Forty Degrees South Pty Ltd

A B O U T

THE SECRET CURRENCY

THE SECRET CURRENCY series brings together unique and innovative ways of business management that lay the foundation for a healthy work life balance that anyone can use. Navigating the Secret Currency, much the same as in life, requires a logical mind, thorough planning, implementation, and review. The Secret Currency will expose some vital experiences that will help to underpin your successful business and satisfying life.

Other books ie series are:
BENNY ADAMS DISCOVERS THE SECRET CURRENCY
POWER OF YOUR THINKING

ACKNOWLEDGEMENTS

Writing this book has, of course, been quite an adventure with inherent ups and downs. It has drawn upon the strengths and resources of many people to whom I am greatly indebted. But, naturally there are those whose added input has meant the difference between planning to 'write something one day' and actually getting it done. Therefore it is to my three talented, supportive and farsighted daughters that I extend my most sincere and loving thanks. Without their care and input this would have been a dream unfulfilled.

I must also give great acknowledgement to my friend, many time advisor, and perpetual sounding board, Steve Major a well-respected and renowned world-stage speaker. Thank you for all your timely advice and opinions. They have been greatly appreciated.

Close on two decades ago I met an interesting person who challenged my traditional thinking and opened my eyes to the endless opportunities of creating wealth. What I have learned from him has set me on my path to success. To John Wolfe my sincere thanks.

CONTENTS

INTRODUCTION

Having been in some form of business, mainly real estate and consultancy, for over three decades now, I have seen and experienced many diverse forms of success and setback. I have seen the 'boom and bust' cycles, the high waves of success followed by the hugely destructive dumpers that have levelled and destroyed businesses and people from all walks of life. Sometimes I have been the dispassionate observer, and at other times I have been more closely involved than I care to remember. But on each occasion I have noticed that there are some savvy citizens out there who seem to remain unscathed by the vagaries of fortune and the ups and downs of markets, rates, exchanges and trends. I have discovered their secrets and actions. I have called these savvy operators the enlightened – the ones who seem to exist in a world where none of the bad times stick.

What I discovered was most interesting and not necessarily related to the factors or features outlined in many self-help books that try to evaluate a person's actions including how these actions relate to acquiring or losing wealth. These enlightened among us seem to be inoculated against disaster on account of certain distinct and frequently recurring factors. And once I realized this I knew I had a responsibility to unveil the invisible cloak of success.

From birth our environment dictates our outward perception. We interpret and rationalize the world forming identities and establishing norms that help to shape our attitudes and actions. What becomes the normal as we perceive it is a reflection of social habit that is 'the same old, same old' ways taught to us from the text books of tradition. They are a clandestine repetition of the faults and floors of past teachings that have become entrenched in our lives causing us to dismiss them as being usual, normal and worse still correct.

Naturally, we are adverse to the unknown and we easily dismiss these thoughts and actions as radical. Yet, the learned minority that walk a thin line between acceptance and disdain are in fact those enlightened ones among us. The revolutionary methods that every once in a while sprout up like mushrooms to change the world as we know it occasionally find merit as they become accepted as authority by the rest of us.

But what if instead of ignoring those voices we instead stop to take a moment and question the traditional ways that have informed our understanding through our entire lives? By allowing yourself to learn the secrets behind the brick wall that once stood in the way of success reserved only for the inventors, we can all access the highly successful systems, methods, and developed behaviors that are being used by the Enlightened. They have amassed great mental wealth that has enabled them to generate other material forms of wealth simply from re-learning the why's and how's of the system.

Social acceptance of a previously radical concept is sometimes all that it takes to generate a valid and normal situation.

Once I became familiar with the functions, uses and applications, there was no turning back to the ways of my past and now, after fifteen years of following the path to self enlightenment, I am ready to share the secret with you and help you prepare for the worlds' financial crises. This is your opportunity to capitalize on the events that will leave others destroyed.

The Secret Currency series brings together unique and innovative ways of business management that lay the foundation for a healthy work life balance that anyone can use. Navigating the Secret Currency, much the same as in life, requires a logical mind, thorough planning, implementation, and review. The Secret Currency will expose some vital experiences that will help to underpin your successful business and satisfying life.

In light of the economic disposition many of us are now faced with, The Secret Currency: Leveraging your Business with Barter is dedicated to informing you of the ways, processes, and approaches of using barter as an alternate currency in an unsure economic climate. This book takes a practical and methodical approach to everyday business quagmires and will map out the many and various practical measures you can employ instantly to improve your situation for the long term.

CHAPTER ONE

AT THE MERCY OF MARKETS

Victory is sweetest when you've known defeat.

—Anon

As a business owner, one is almost always at the mercy of the markets and its ups and downs. This was never more so than with the Great Depression of the 1930s. Riding on the heels of one of the world's most severe humanitarian catastrophes, people were left with nowhere to turn and the images of people jumping from the windows of city skyscrapers continues to haunt the market to this very day. Real estate prices dived to unimaginable lows and there appeared to be a very grim future ahead for everyone. The global impact of the economic meltdown caused unimaginable personal and professional hardship and the remnants of the Great Depression cast an eerie legacy across down markets.

For some it wasn't so much about the loss of funds, although that was devastating in itself, it was about the loss of pride, the loss of renown as a good business owner and manager. It was about the shame of becoming a loser after having been a winner for so long. All too often It Is this shame and embarrassment, or the fear of it that drives a lot of business owners to desperate lengths and even more desperate actions and reactions.

More recently we have seen the effects of the global credit crunch and its effects on business, banking, real estate, the stock market and financial confidence all round. The devastation it wreaked was almost comparable to that of the 1930s, save for the injection of the multi-billion dollar stimulus packages.

THE MONEY MARKET

The flow-on effects of the sub-prime mortgage collapse have been swift and without precedent. For years housing purchasers with poor to medium credit ratings had been encouraged to take out impossible loans, being promised that their vulnerability and exposure would decrease with time, given the continuing boom in the housing industry and the real-estate market. But the market didn't continue to grow. And re-payments didn't get easier over time. In fact, there soon emerged the worrying trend of having so many foreclosures in the market that the banks' revenue was being severely threatened. This meant that, in essence the banks had little to lend and credit availability was suddenly reduced. All of the cash injections from other countries and from other markets suddenly seemed to disappear.

All at once, investors panicked too and the global stock markets suffered huge declines. All over the world, economies slowed to a crawl as credit became less available. International trade also took a severe hit. The stock index was down by a massive 45%.

No wonder, people were running scared at every turn. Everyone that is except for the CEOs being paid millions of dollars per year as wage and incentives packages. It soon became apparent that these cash grabbing managers and CEOs had been unfettered and unchecked for years. It seemed that not surprisingly, the Emperor's new clothes were more than apparent.

The middle class, working class of the western world were walking half naked in the streets, wretched with loss and lack of prospects, while the individuals who had seemingly caused the crisis in the first place, by being too free with the availability of credit, had only the comfort of millions of dollars to protect them. It was a contrast that was not lost on the governments of developed countries and one which was going to suffer great changes.

President Obama bailed out industry after failing industry to the tune of billions of dollars only to see those bail-out packages being funneled into the personal accounts of the CEOs and directors. There had to be massive changes – in writing, in law.

The money markets were all set to just pick up where they had left off and keep going in the same vein as they had always done, but President Obama had other ideas. And so another plummet in the markets in the beginning of 2010 echoed the ever jittery tensions on Wall Street.

The bull and the bear are at constant odds in the money market but their struggle is nothing compared to the real-life repercussions for the everyday trader and business owner. In fact, the push for mom and pop investors in the last twenty years of the twentieth century saw many invest their life savings, basically betting that the bull would beat the bear at every turn, and for some time, while markets were high, they were lulled into erroneous beliefs that they would win. And they did. The financial world was rife with the stories and rumors, exaggerated or not, about little mom and pop investors who had put in their few thousand and emerged millionaires. It seemed too good to be true – and where there is the breaking story of a gold rush, there are plenty of gullible people to follow.

Soon everyone was wanting to ride the winning stock markets, not thinking that there was the remotest possibility that things could go so badly wrong – the 1980s had shown us all how easy it was to get rich and live wonderfully well. But the 1990s had a few surprises in store for the financial markets – but still the mom and pop investors stayed around. Many pulled out when they began to sustain some losses, but by and large, fuelled by the information given to them by 'financial advisors', many small time investors, decided to stay in the game and ride the bull for all it was worth.

Come the 2000s and the bull was seen in very few places. Come 2007-2008-2009, the bull was almost nonexistent and only those riding the dollar down on the back of the bear had anything to be smiling about. No-body could have predicted the 45% loss in the markets. It was to be a horrendous blow.

With the *credit crunch*, these investors, if they hadn't been totally wiped out, left in such numbers that they would never again return to the supposedly risky, volatile markets that can elevate and decimate at any tick of the clock.

The bail outs, the fiscal stimulus, the amended monetary policies, the wavering stock markets, all symbolic of investor temerity, all centered around credit ratings and credit availability, at times, they seemed to be mere inert phrases incapable of producing any real remediation or securing future progress. And yet, little by little the change came. The stock-market seemed to quiet a little of the hysterical shrieks and settled down to a modicum of normality that was able to comfort investors.

But the truth is, even when one has recovered from disaster, when one is seated upon a new throne surveying a new kingdom, the ravages of the past are never very far away, and sentiment is never as buoyant or innocent again. And in 2011 the same thing happened again. The United States was in melt-down after its first credit rating downgrade in history. The markets panicked and billions have been lost in the share markets … again.

THE REAL ESTATE MARKET

Use your leverage. Use your equity. Use your credit cards. Go Platinum. Use your home as extra collateral – there's no risk. The price of real-estate doubles every 10 years. There's heaps of credit for those who want to take advantage. There's no such thing as bad debt. Be smart. Make it happen for you. We have all the money you will need to set up a new business. Need renovations? We can lend you the money. Come and see us. There is so much easy credit available that you can virtually have as much as you want. And then there is always the possibility of a great line of credit to use. Don't use your cash. And what about a reverse mortgage? Safe as houses.

For so long the average home-owner and business owner were harangued and plied with such sophisticated advertising that they came to believe in the hype of easy credit and long term repayments that would barely be noticeable. They believed that this was what life was like in the affluent new age. This is how they were supposed to live and living the good life was their right and almost obligatory.

Accountants set up the right kind of funding options and accounts and soon the flow of money was so strong there was no stopping it. It became almost normal for middle-class, middle-aged home-owners to have three or more homes, all rented out, all being paid for by someone else and it all seemed to be rolling along nicely.

It was nothing for business owners to use their home(s) as collateral and everyone was supposed to live happily ever after. Who knew that it would all end so disastrously – well the bankers should have known, the governments should have known, the IMF should have known – and yet the Emperor continued to wear his new clothes with glee and admiration from all.

And then … B 0 0 M ! The bubble burst so loudly and with such ferocity that its reverberations were felt all around the world. All of a sudden foreclosures were the flavor of the month and there were so many of them, the market went into free fall. You could buy a house for a fraction of what it was once worth. And with the drop in interest rates, you would be mad not to – save for the fact that you had already been totally destroyed by now from the banks and money lenders calling in loans left right and centre. No-one told you that in the small print, they didn't have to give you notice – they can call in a loan at any time they choose, even if your payments are up to date and current.

It was a time of trauma, insecurity and devastation that the housing market had never seen before, save for the Great Depression of the 1930s. And here it was, happening at a time that was supposed to be prosperous, hopeful and full of prospects. Accountants, lawyers, small business operators, home-owners, pensioners, doctors, teachers – the ones who were normally supposed to be immune from these types of pressures and influences, were all standing in the unemployment lines along with everyone else. And they were in the soup-kitchens and charity shops along with the working poor. Demand on social services had never been so great.

SUPERANNUATION OR 401K SAFETY NET

And what is there to be said for superannuation or 401K benefits? Weren't they supposed to bail us out when we got into difficulties? There was a way out after all. People in their droves went to access their accounts, comforted by the knowledge that there was a back up. There was a plan that could bail them out.

This was the exact thing that they had protected themselves from. This was the reason they had taken out the policies. Now it was time to cash them in. Alas, panic set in once more - the 401K was dependent on the stock market and its ups and downs to determine the returns one would receive.

And as the stock market had gone into free fall and wiped out billions of dollars in stock and shares – the resulting profits in 401K returns were also wiped out. For many funds substantial losses meant that almost half of the invested monies were lost. And to add insult to injury, red tape that extended to unprecedented lengths prevented people accessing the funds anyway.

For no apparent reason at all, except that people became very nervous, very fast, billions were wiped out. And thousands of lives were devastated and destroyed. Countless stories of families living on the streets, empty houses being sold for a third of their previous value, unavailability of jobs, lack of consumer confidence and much more made this an overwhelming global disaster.

There were some very loud voices in the wilderness crying out before all of this took place. There were some very influential commentators, business owners and operators, Peter Schiff and Robert Kiyosaki among them, who were bemoaning the state of affairs at least three years before the collapse took place. But like Noah and his Ark, no-body believed them until the rain started to fall, and then of course it was too late for most.

THE VALUE OF MONEY

In 1970 Richard Nixon made a fiscal decision that would have detrimental and ominous effects that would ripple through the future of the western world. He declared that the US dollar would no longer be backed by gold value, but would become a currency in its own right, a *fiat* currency – with no real value to support it. In essence it gave the United States the ability to print as much paper currency as it chose backed substantially by nothing of real value. And so it did, and for a while it seemed to be working. But with no substance behind it, it was soon susceptible to the same volatile and feeble influences that affected the rest of the world markets. It has declined in value ever since that time.

With nothing solid to support the dollar during the *credit crunch*, the values were naturally set to fall. There was nothing to hold it, sustain it or to guard it. And in the end the whole world suffered as a result.

It is no wonder that we allow ourselves to be at the mercy of whoever has hold of the reigns. We don't know that there are any alternatives. We allow ourselves to believe that we are just the sheep, the pawns or the small players who have no choice. And in the long run, we are exactly where we are meant to be – on the board playing the role envisaged by the bankers.

It would all be just a fine intellectual exercise if it weren't for the fact that real people with real losses and real business collapses were suffering at the hands of the drivers.

These days in schools, children are taught about the environment and how to protect it. They are taught about recycling and energy efficiency and waste reduction and water conservation. By the time they are in high school they know more about reducing their carbon foot-print than their parents do. They know about global warming and how to stay the effects. However, they have no voice, no collective voice at least, with which to boast of their wisdom or with which to convince the policy makers.

Children know too, that in the future they will likely have to be responsible for their own domestic power supply, their own water collection, storage and usage and probably, their own food production, at least partially. This is the direction in which the world is heading and the children at least, are preparing for it. They know what they have to do and they are practicing their skills already.

And what is to be said for the mature adults among us? In theory we know all of the above and expect it all to take shape sooner or later, but many of us still believe that we can go on living our energy rich lifestyles with minimal repercussions! Sound familiar? Substitute the phrase 'energy rich' with financially rich, and we'll have the perfect scenario for another *credit crunch*.

If there was to be no electricity to power the houses next year, and we knew that, and we planned for that, wouldn't we be considered plain stupid if we didn't take compensatory steps to allow us to embrace and develop other methods of power supply? So when the chop came, and there was a failing of power, we would have planned for it and made alternative arrangements for it. We would have planned for our lives to be able to go on without the regular supply. The new supply may not have all the bells and whistles we had been accustomed to, but it still did the job. It still supplied enough power for us to be able to live our lives.

And so it is with money – if we knew there was a time coming, when there would be very little of it available or if we knew that a time was coming when there would be different 'strings' attached to it, then would we not make alternative arrangements so that when the 'crunch' came we could go on living our lives, albeit not as luxuriously as before, but happily enough?

So many make the mistake of thinking that savings, mutual funds, hedge funds and the like are the only alternatives for planning for a time of shortage. What they don't realize is that with money, not being backed by anything solid, is subject to the fluctuations of the market – hence, what you thought was $1,000 cash in your saving account could be worth 45% less in the next *credit crunch*. So, apart from buying shares in gold, silver and oil, which is what the big boys do, the only other intelligent option for the everyday business owner is to use another form of money, and conserve the cash flow s/he has.

COULD THE USE OF BARTER HAVE PREVENTED THE CREDIT CRUNCH?

This is a very interesting question and not as ridiculous as it may first appear. In a word, no, it could not have prevented it, but definitely yes, it could have prevented the absolute devastation that was sustained by so many smaller operatives.

It has often been said that during times of financial downturn, barter use is at its highest. And no wonder. When cash is tight, then the natural and normal human reaction is to hold on to it as long we can. But for the most part, business owners will try to hang on to it to save their business. What they don't realize is, that by trying to hold on to cash, and trying to save their business, they can, ultimately be destroying the very thing they want to preserve.

Take the following scenario for instance – Andreas is a small business deli owner. During times of economic downturn, people aren't willing to pay $70 per kilo for prosciutto when they can make do with $3 per kilo bacon. They don't want buffalo mozzarella when a slice of cheddar will suffice. In fact grocery staples become much more basic as the financial squeeze gained momentum. Andreas hasn't heard of barter and keeps thinking this downturn won't last long. He's ridden out the storms before and this is just another passing phase.

Sharon, just over the road from Andreas, also owns a deli – with more of an Asian twist, but still stocks all the Italian sausage and antipasto items at the same prices and has the same overheads.

Sharon is equally susceptible to the financial markets and their swings. Sharon however, has heard of barter. She has been using it for some time and knows the ins and outs of it. She knows how to use it to her advantage. Instead of just hoping to ride out the storm, Sharon has put up proverbial shutters to make her business immune to the shock. She is not expecting to sustain any damages.

Sharon uses barter to its maximum potential by exploring avenues to access barter before utilizing her cash reserves. For instance, she chooses to pay for staff rewards and incentives, bookkeeping and accountant's fees, supplies and marketing solutions. This small difference in detail between them has meant that instead of downsizing, Sharon is now expecting business growth. Instead of being affected by the financial downturn as with everyone else, she actually starts to see a rise in returns and has been able to keep her staff in work, provide business to her suppliers and keep things ticking along nicely, all thanks to utilizing alternative currency to leverage her business.

Andreas, like many business owners within two months of the *credit crunch* had closed his doors for good – after 25 years of selling his wares. Andreas' failure to plan for the worst meant that he too would fall victim to the false reality created by fiat currency.

FOR THE BUSINESS OWNER, WHAT DOES THIS ALL MEAN?

It's easy to be glib after the fact. It's easy to have 20-20 hindsight vision – all of that is easy and totally irrelevant to the pain and disaster that everyday business owners have endured as a result of this credit crunch. We can't undo what has now been done as a result of the *credit crunch*, but what happens when the next disaster strikes? What of the average business owner then? What happens to him or her when the winds of fortune change for the worse again?

To simply say that one has to be prepared is mind-numbingly annoying, but in its purest form this is the best solution. Glib and monotonously repetitive sayings such as 'a stitch in time saves nine' or 'prevention is better than cure', can do more harm than good. They just re-enforce feelings of failure and loss. To be truly helpful one has to understand the depths of despair from which those who have lost their wherewithal have come. But these sayings are overused and common and have become battering rams, because they are true!

To the business owner who doesn't have the safety net of a barter system upon which to rely or fall back upon, it can be a perilous journey ahead. It can and possibly will be more of the same – the ups the downs, the terror, the fear of not knowing. Unless you're in a particularly enviable position, then you will not be able to avoid the calamities of future upsets. If major companies like General Motors can almost go to the wall, then what chance does a small to medium business have? The joke of course is that the bigger the business, the greater the possibility of being bailed out by the government of the day. But, when you're just a little fish flapping about gasping for life, saviors seem to be few and far between.

That's why the added comfort of knowing about and using barter to your advantage can be a huge salve to a struggling business. It's no surprise that barter use is at its highest during tough times. That's one of the reasons it was invented.

KNOWING YOUR BUSINESS' PLACE IN THE OPERATING ENVIRONMENT

The pure essence of vision is the thrill of watching the fruits of your labor turn into magnificent successes. It's the stuff of dreams and legends. And what great business man or woman didn't have an inspiring dream behind them to raise their spirits and keep them going when things got tough? But the vision can all too quickly turn into a blinding nightmare when the efforts that have gone into realizing the vision, suddenly produce less than desired results. We have already talked about the number of seriously real things that can and do go wrong for the unwary or inexperienced business owner.

The demands on the availability of the dollar are relentless and regular. Every day, every week, every month there are outgoings that must be honored. Every day, week and month there are incomings that should cover them. But more often than not, in the first five years, the incomings fall short of the outgoings and business failure and/or financial ruin is the result – at least for 80% of new businesses.

Now more than ever, it is vital to call a spade a spade and recognize the realities that are facing your business and your future. Ostriches cannot survive in this environment. Hiding, ignoring, pretending it isn't happening, waiting for the storm clouds to lift, none of these approaches work – in fact, if anything, they make things significantly worse.

For instance – Elspeth owns a shoe store – it is one of two in the town and hers is the one in the better location, close to the pedestrian traffic with banks, cafes and so on. She has the best range of shoes in the entire region and spends thousands per month on television, radio and print ads. She is always supporting other businesses in the town and actively promotes shopping in the precinct. She is head of several retailers committees and has been the figurehead behind many accomplishments within the retail sector of the town.

But Elspeth, unbeknownst to others in the town, is almost broke. She hangs on for Christmas and back-to-school rushes and these two events are what sustain her, almost. As she drives about town in her late model BMW she is the epitome of the successful businesswoman, even being the Vice President of the local Chamber of Commerce, giving others advice on how to run their business.

Only to a trusted few does she unburden her troubles – only to these trusted friends does she dare talk about her impending ruin. She wakes through the night several times, shaking with the dread of the IRS, unpaid suppliers, car re-possessors and advertising companies taking her to court and suing her for unpaid fees. The night terrors set her up for nervous days, avoiding phone calls and sending red letters to her also unpaid accountant. And then she shrugs and says 'I guess I'm just not a very good business woman!' and continues on as before.

But little by little the mountain of unpaid bills grows and little by little she is falling deeper into the hole. During the *credit crunch*, she was about to close her doors for good, but pride wouldn't let her. She can't sell the business because the books are too bad to secure a good selling price. She has gone on like this for at least three years. There is no telling how much longer she can sustain the pretence.

It's time she took the blinkers off! It's time she saw her business, warts and all for what it really is. She has sought business advice. She has listened to it. She has read about it. She has engaged consultants. But she has never acted. It's as if there is a great wall that is preventing her from moving into the winning circle.

What's that old saying about the lobster on the rock? If it only knew it had to move but a few inches into the water to be saved! But instead, it sits on the rock, immovable waiting to die. What nonsense when business owners do the same thing.

The business owner, like Elspeth in the face of the oncoming storm, could immediately make some significant changes that would turn things around for the business. Measures taken in this circumstance could include:

- Re-evaluate employee returns – determine if your staff are fulfilling or exceeding their obligations or are they simply letting the business down? Many employers are shy when it comes to staffing issues. You shouldn't be afraid to take charge. Know your industry obligations and do what is best for your business, even if that means having to let wayward staff go.
- Re-evaluate advertising channels – regular media is costly, although you still need to keep a level of presence in the industry, try to balance your advertising with more cost effective methods such as online media – if you are new to this concept you should seek the advice of a consultant. Where possible try to maximize

your barter dollars here as you could easily turn barter into cash by attracting new business.

- Re-evaluate your stock-on-hand and return or sell any excess stock where possible. Putting the cash back into your account will help you through hard times where as lay-around stock will not. You could even opt to sell your excess stock through barter, building your reserves which could be used to pay for other services your business demands - such as accountants, bookkeepers and advertising.

- In this day and age you would be a dime a dozen if you weren't already capitalizing upon your online market potential. Having an online store gives your pre-existing customers more flexibility in the way they interact with your business and will attract a wider market as you can now cater to the needs of people beyond your geographical location – you could even establish a successful niche for your market across the other side of the country.

One of the largest mistakes that a business owner could make when the market shows signs of slowing down is to not re-evaluate their business soon enough. By looking for and cutting out the waste in every area of your business (you cannot be soft about this either) and by leveraging you business on the readily available market of barter, things could turn around pretty fast and you would be far better prepared to ride the wave when it comes and goes. Moving beyond the traditional ways of doing business in a cash market and exploring newer, smarter ways of doing business is the best exercise in business planning you could do. And it works!

SIGNS TO LOOK OUT FOR

For the vast majority of the 80% who fail in new businesses, remediation was possible. Help was available. The ever present curse of the lack of or non-existent cash flow was curable. The lack of budget for advertising was possible to attain through non cash based sources.

Be prepared. Take corrective action. Make massive changes. Take charge. Be in control of your business' destiny. Devise and use the plan that works best for any business during any economic environment. There is not a magic wand that some businesses have access to and others don't. There is no secret club or society that helps some and not others, not one that will prevent your success.

Once you start hearing or making excuses such as:

- When the economy recovers.
- When winter is over.
- When summer is over.
- When the tourists return.
- When the dollar gets stronger.
- When the dollar gets weaker.
- When the cost of supplies drops.
- When … when … when.

It's at this point when you've begun to lose the battle. All good business owners have and use a plan that encompasses all likely eventualities. True there are some curve balls that hit you square on, and you sure didn't see them coming, but a good business is resilient enough to adapt, adjust and keep performing. The following chapters explores in detail the techniques, methods and adaptations that are necessary for the establishment, development and continued growth of a thriving business – all with one difference – the use of alternative currencies like barter.

CHAPTER ONE

SUMMARY

- There are no assured safety nets in business apart from forward thinking and planning. You must make your own safety nets according to your business strengths. Many business owners don't have a 401K believing the worth of their business at retirement will be sufficient.

- Modern business ventures and management encompass the use of cash as well as alternative currencies.

- Barter is an intelligent way to manage cash flow and P&L.

- Actively assessing the true nature of your situation is the first step to turning your business around and surviving cash shortages.

- Preparing for likely eventualities by identifying and responding to certain business indicators.

CHAPTER TWO

THE POWER OF LEVERAGE

*We're looking to have the ability to come in and be able to
capitalize on the marketing in order to grow the top-line.
We basically leverage what has worked with our other
successful acquisitions – investment in marketing,
retention and student services.*

—John Larson

In many business books and courses and MBAs and the like, there is often talk about 'leverage'. But what is it in terms that everyone can understand? Why would you need a college education to understand its meaning and its ramifications? When you do a rudimentary search for the term you are inundated with complicated, industry specific explanations that rely on jargon, detailed financial and investing knowledge and applications that can be confusing and misleading.

Some financial 'educators' become so caught up in the intricacies and minutiae of the term, that many business owners who would benefit greatly from a broad understanding of the concept are permanently turned off learning about leverage, and what's more they are also turned off the idea of learning more about the possibilities of becoming more successful as a result of using leverage.

So, in general terms, what is it and how can it benefit your business? By using the old fulcrum and lever example, you get to see how the concept actually works. And in fact, the term leverage uses the word 'lever' as its root. And a lever, as we all know is a rod, bar, stick, arm that is rigid and resting on a pivot. You are able to move a load by applying pressure to the end of the lever. So, leverage is when you are able to gain a positive result that is greater than the result you would have achieved without the use of a lever. In other words, you are able to move a bigger load with the use of a lever, than you would have been able to move without it.

A lever, or leverage, was one of the most basic tools or mechanisms ever used – and to this day remains as one of the most powerful ways to extend a small effort for a big result.

It's easy to see how this works on a practical level, but how does it work in a business model? Financially the term has long been associated with using borrowed money to make an investment that will return profits that are greater than the interest payable. In terms of growing your business, it's about finding ways that you can get more profit out of lesser effort. Think about a Hollywood star for example. They get leverage because each time their movie is shown, their celebrity and influence increase, their popularity grows and their fees for performing go up. That's how we get actors who can command over a million dollars for one performance. That is leverage at its best.

If you have a book that is a success then you also get great leverage. You don't have to rely on just one book being sold, you are leveraging your talent each time you sell a book – so the book that is on the *New York Times* bestseller list is probably guaranteed to sell tens of thousands of copies, if not hundreds of thousands. And so your leverage grows and the next time you want to write a book, your leverage is already strong and you can command more and more as an up-front fee and your royalty deals will be better each time. This is also why a youth worker or receptionist can never get enough leverage to attract more capital. They are what they are – fairly isolated without recourse to greater funds because of their limited status. And generally, they can never increase their leverage because their level of influence is not that great – if they want to use leverage they will have to operate in a completely different way.

In the case of a business, if you are able to extend your credibility, raise your profile, become a household name and be recognized as a brand within your own right, then your ability to bring in more money, attract investors, expand your operation and grow your business, increases exponentially.

THE NEED FOR LEVERAGE

Once you figure out the reasoning behind the process it's pretty easy to see why leverage is so vital to the growth of a business. In the general business world there are six ways in which leverage is used to advance any business:

1 Investment from outside sources.
2 Using the knowledge of industry experts.
3 Making the most of innovative ideas.
4 Other people's talent.
5 Other people's time.
6 Barter and alternative currencies.

Making intelligent use of these methods is the way that smart business owners get ahead fast. It's worth a closer look to see how this is achieved.

INVESTMENT FROM OUTSIDE SOURCES

This involves being able to attract, beg or borrow money from places that are not your own. For example, this happens routinely when you buy real estate. You put a small percent down as a deposit, and borrow the remainder. In essence the lending body is the person that owns the property, but you are the one who has control over the property – you are responsible for maintaining it and paying for it and abides by the laws of the land in relation to it, much the same as the rights and obligations that exist under a lease. You have leveraged someone else's money to get what you want. Attracting investors into your business or company also works in the same way, although there would be other conditions that apply to this type of investment.

USING THE KNOWLEDGE OF INDUSTRY EXPERTS

This is an intangible way of leveraging your business. Using the notion of learning from other people's mistakes has long been a way of improving your own business. If for instance, you are having trouble with a particular aspect of your product or service, and you know that Company X has already found a solution to the problem and you are able to access the solution then, you would be crazy to ignore the knowledge that you can easily gain. This is why there is mentoring, coaching, motivational speaking. It's all about keeping the momentum going in your own business while taking advantage of the knowledge gained from other people's / businesses' failures. Knowing what steps to take and what paths to avoid is a great way of taking your business to higher levels, without having to endure the agony and limitations of learning everything for yourself. You are leveraging knowledge – to better your business skills.

MAKING THE MOST OF INNOVATIVE IDEAS

Knowing your market position and the business and economic climate that surround it requires you to play a watchdog role. Keeping a close ear to the forums, associations, articles, reports, books, magazines and the like and listening to what others are saying and doing, filtering the information for something that will give your business the advantage it needs. This may be an abstract concept for a small business owner however, the key to taking your product sales from mediocre to skyrocketing success, involves a holistic approach to developing cutting edge business success.

OTHER PEOPLE'S TALENT

No matter how hard we try, we can only ever squeeze 24 hours out of one day. It doesn't get longer or shorter – a day is a day and if you are like the rest of the world's busy business owners, you will know this more keenly than most. That is why so many smart and successful business owners leverage their time. Their day is actually worth 10 or two or six days of the ordinary person's time. How? They surround themselves with experts – experts for hire. They hire or employ those people who have the answers to problems they can't solve. And usually it is cheaper to hire these people on an ad hoc basis than it is to try and solve the problems alone. Hiring someone who is capable and dedicated to study of sector specific phenomena and is able to transform research, studies, surveys, user satisfaction tests and the like into beneficial outcomes could save you an enormous amount of time and produce great results for your business very quickly. You don't have to be the expert in every aspect of your business, you just have to know which direction you want to take your business and generally how you would like to get there. You also need to know that your foot is responsible for the accelerator and the speed at which you arrive at your destination.

OTHER PEOPLE'S TIME

Not everyone wants to be in business. Not everyone wants to be an entrepreneur. Not everyone wants the responsibility of being the boss. For most people in fact, the most that they want is to have a job and build a life from that job. Leverage your time by hiring someone to do all those jobs you don't want to do – if it doesn't thrill you, give it to some that does get a thrill from it.

BARTER

This last form of leverage is one that is often neglected, overlooked or even unknown to many business owners. This is the leverage you gain when you preserve your cash flow and use barter dollars for as many of your business expenses as you can. This is the way that a number of smaller businesses grow so quickly into bigger businesses. This is probably one of the most important ways to leverage your money, your time and your talent – you would be surprised how many businesses such as accountants, lawyers, advisors and the like use barter so you don't have to use your cash.

Leverage is something that often gets forgotten when you are so bogged down in the day to day doing of things that seem so essential. There are a myriad of excuses that a business owner puts up because basically he or she is afraid – and the list of fears is long. There is the fear of failure, the fear of success, the fear of dealing with other people, the fear of rejection, the fear of criticism, the fear of being ridiculed for trying and so on. This is why you hear so many successful business owners saying that they have spent as much money and time on their mindset as they have on their business expenses. Leveraging their attitudes is a big part of their success or failure.

LEVERAGING YOUR MINDSET

Whether we like to admit it or not, most of us are unequivocally the product of our upbringing and entrenched standards and morals. If you have been raised to believe that it's OK to cheat your neighbor, your customer or your family, then this will be the type of attitude that will be reflected in your business. If you believe that life was meant to be hard, that business was meant to be harder and that life never gives a sucker an even break, then this will also be reflected in your business, whether you think it is or not. If, on the other hand you believe that life if good, that the opportunity of a lifetime comes along every week, and that basically people are good and honest, then this will be your business persona. The business owner who is intent on screwing the last cent out of his customers, will also be doing the same to his staff and his suppliers. It is a mindset that rules all of his behaviors and it is the same mindset that shapes how others think of him.

What you think, how you think and what you believe to be true for you, will be reflected in all aspects of your business, from the time-sheet to your Policies and Procedures Manual. And ultimately what you give out comes back to you in one form or another.

So if it's all going to be a reflection of you and your attitudes and beliefs, then wouldn't it be better to spend some time leveraging the good bits that will come back to you. Decide on the values and principles that you want your business to reflect – and then work on implementing them into your own behaviors. New habits can be hard to establish, and that is why some sort of mentorship or peer motivational support is so important.

But as far as leveraging is concerned, the best way to leverage your attitudes is to insist on them forming part of your modus operandi. Have them as part of your mission statement. Insist on an employee code of conduct, and keep your people accountable.

CHAPTER TWO

SUMMARY

- Slow and steady does not win the race. If you want to build your business fast you have to utilize leverage. Make it work for you, your business, your attitudes and your prosperity.

- Being the boss doesn't mean you have to be the expert in every aspect of your business. Leverage your knowledge and skills by hiring others with the knowledge you lack.

- Leverage your time by not wasting it doing things you can hire others to do.

- Leverage your industry smarts, by hiring others who are passionate about your industry.

- Leverage your skills by employing the expert skills of others.

- Leverage your time by employing others to do the things that you don't like to do – the things that waste your time and keep you from income producing activity.

- Leverage your cash flow by using barter dollars to preserve cash.

- Leverage your mindset by sorting the wheat from the tares – discard the baggage that no longer serves you well and move on to bigger and better things.

CHAPTER THREE

THE CONCEPT OF BARTER

*All government, indeed every human benefit and
enjoyment, every virtue, and every prudent act, is founded
on compromise and barter.*
—Edmund Burke

Is there some sort of secret that some successful businesses have that other's don't? Many would argue that success is in the detail, in the planning, in the objectification of the processes, in the removal of personality and heart. Others would argue that luck and good fortune just seem to be attracted to certain individuals. Indeed we all seem to know someone to whom this sort of luck could be attributed.

Over 80% of new businesses fail within the first five years! That's a great statistic to motivate you into a new venture – and if you're already in, then you know how fast you have to paddle and bail just to keep things afloat – and then of course there are the times, when you're not quite afloat at all. That's when you're swimming for all you're worth just to keep your head above water.

But if you've worked hard and planned well and made all the right moves to the bank and other bodies, you may be doing well enough. And well enough is good enough for a while until some strange phenomenon such as the global credit crunch hits you like a bolt from the blue and sends your business into a tailspin – and not only that, your personal assets take a hit too.

But what if there were another factor at play that many people didn't know about, or didn't know enough about? What if it were *this* factor that was the stabilizing influence in both the start-up and growth stages of a business? What if this advantage were available to all businesses? Well in a nutshell – here it is – barter.

WHAT IS BARTER?

It is at this initial stage that many people are 'turned off' before they discover the advantages that are available to them. Many ask the questions but care not to heed learned advice. We've all met someone like this at some stage in our lives.

The basic form of barter, or trading, is as old as Methuselah. If my chickens were laying well and I had extra eggs, I may consider giving you some eggs, that you don't have, for a few bananas that I don't have and you do. There are many businesses today that still operate in this way to some degree or another. For instance, I will exchange the catering order you want from my restaurant for some tweaking of my electrical systems in the kitchen, from your electrical business.

The introduction of an objective party, such as a network or facilitator, enables equitable indirect transaction. The intermediary is allied to no other business operator by industry therefore allowing the whole process to be streamlined and made more equitable. And this is exactly what has happened to the modern barter industry. There are barter exchanges where trade coordinators take care of business accounts. So, the development of the barter industry now by and large looks something like this:

- Barter is wanted by businesses to help offset cash costs and get rid of excess stock to other businesses. There are times when it is easier, more frugal, more profitable and more sensible to exchange goods and services for other goods and services. Having an objective and equitable way of doing that is desirable.
- Equitable systems must maintain operational fairness in order to provide any significant value – with the introduction of a formalized barter system, all parties can be guaranteed an equitable settlement

on transactions and no one party need ever go away feeling they had been dealt a raw deal.

- Objective third parties, brokers or coordinators overseeing trans-actions immediately cleared the way for better, more transparent transactions. As goods and services are valued at the same level as goods and services in the retail sector there is less possibility of bias or under/overcharging.
- All barter transactions to take place according to agreed terms.
- A barter dollar equals a local currency dollar.
- Nominal interest is paid in cash to the broker for processing of transactions while a portion of services is paid for with the use of barter.
- Monthly statements are issued – just as it is imperative to keep a close and organized eye upon cash flow and statements, the same is possible for barter dollars, ensuring an intelligent, objective system that enables bookkeepers and accountants alike to keep track of transactions and P&L amounts.

Promotion of businesses within a network is encouraged and is free – one of the most valuable assets within a barter network is the way in which brokerages interact in order to promote the business of any member throughout the country – as a service to members.

Naturally it is in everyone's best interest to have all businesses trading and exchanging and trading goods and services. Cash customers are enticed to purchase with real dollars when they can see businesses interacting with one another in trust. There is no greater promotion for a business than the recommendation of a satisfied customer. It doesn't matter that a customer is a barter customer or not. All that really matters is that a business transaction has taken place and each party is satisfied with the outcome.

All barter dollars are regarded as cash dollars according to IRS regulation standards and as such are subject to the same deductions and costs. At times there have been moans and groans from reticent businesses regarding barter, suggesting that when it came to tax time, it was impossible to factor in the barter effect and the barter dollars that had been traded in and out of the account. In practice though, with trade dollars being equal to cash dollars in value, accounting for tax purposes is relatively simple.

FINANCE AND CASH FLOW

The number one reason so many businesses fail is their lack of sufficient funds to keep them afloat. This does not necessarily mean staying afloat only during tough times, this means being able to pay wages, rents, loan repayments, utilities and so on, even in the good times. And the incessant regularity with which they recur can be enough to try even the most stoic of characters.

In starting up a business and ensuring there are sufficient funds to keep the venture afloat and producing cash flow, most businesses don't anticipate the many and varied costs that could be incurred from sources they didn't even consider. Yet once a barter line of credit has been established and is available there are immediately more options open to that business and the strain and demands upon every dollar are immediately ameliorated.

The phrase that 'cash is king' is no less true with the introduction of barter into a business's operations. In fact, it is truer than ever. You can't put food on the table with the promise of payments to come, with the hope of newer, better returns on investment. With the use of barter, there is more cash that is available to the business for the everyday running of things. And with the availability of more cash, the less stress there is on the business owner and the business. There are instantly available greater amounts of cash flow, once barter has been introduced.

The best advice a new business owner can receive is to ensure s/he has enough capital to last at least a year with no returns. If they can do that, then they will go a long way to avoiding the calamitous results some business owners suffer. However, there are few who are able to achieve this sort of result – usually there are bank loans, mortgage repayments and a whole lot of other bills that need regular attention.

But in the very initial stages of setting up a business it is even more basic than that – but still quite as daunting. Some things every start-up business owner has to consider are initial set up fees such as having enough cash flow to pay the accountant, the lawyer, the insurance broker and others. Then there are the fees associated with business registration, domain name registration and hosting, licenses, permits and of course worker's compensation.

Then one has to consider the costs involved with the fit out of premises. There is the age old ogre of rent, deposits, more lawyers' fees, fit out of benches, furniture, point of sale displays, storage and so on. Utilities have to be connected and funded and offices need to be supplied with relevant equipment and stationery. And if you're really lucky, you will also have the added expenses involved in the purchase or hire of heavy equipment, vehicles, telecommunications services and computers and software. There are also the costs involved in purchasing raw materials and other supplies needed for the business.

Working capital is then needed as well as enough cash flow to keep up repayments on all of the above and you haven't even hired staff yet. Oh – and just in case you overlooked this little gem, let's remind you – if you are taking out a loan to fund your business, then chances are the bank will require you to mortgage your home or use it as collateral should you default on your repayments. So, no pressure …

When you consider the vast array of factors competing for the hard earned dollar, then it's no surprise that the initial statistic quoted of 80% of businesses failing within the first five years, is true. Throw a Global Credit crunch into the mix and it's a miracle that anyone has been left standing.

HIRING EMPLOYEES

Hiring new employees can be a nightmare, but regardless of how the business owner goes about this, or regardless too, of how long staff have been in the business, there are ways of using barter to improve your cash flow and still provide your employees with incentives and rewards.

With the use of barter, employees can be gifted a barter card of their own upon which they are free to put charges incurred from holidays, restaurants, clothing, shoes, gifts and so on. The cards are limited to the amount you wish to spend and the employees are able to use them as they see fit.

Many business owners often choose to pay their staff wages with part barter components and if you have a thriving barter network around you most staff are more than happy to oblige.

When it comes to the process of hiring employees, many start-up business owners fall into one of several traps. They either take on someone they know, someone to whom they are related or someone who is the friend of a friend. The other scenario that unfolds is one that results from extensive advertising, complex hiring procedures and extended time lines – in other words the rules and procedures they have established in order to get someone on board are so complex and impossible to achieve, that nearly everyone falls short of requirements. And thus their initial belief that 'good staff are as rare as hen's teeth' is always upheld.

Both of the above types of hiring result from fear – firstly that highly skilled and qualified people will expose the new business owner's lack of expertise in any area and secondly that no-one else, apart from the owner him/herself is capable of successfully doing what needs to be done.

In a majority of cases, the business owner is making the difficult transition from employee to employer and is still in the mindset of a worker – so when it comes time to change hats, it can be a difficult process. Oftentimes, it will be found that the new business owner has to hire and fire a few times before s/he gets into the employer's mindset. They find out that being a buddy as well as the boss, doesn't mix.

The concept of staff incentives and rewards is one which is often bandied about between business owners. Some view them as necessary evils. Some view them as happy recompense for a job well done. Others view them as unnecessary altogether and don't bother with them.

The complications and costs involved with staff training, team-building, goal setting and target accomplishments can be a nightmare in themselves. And this aspect of starting up a business can be a minefield for the new business owner, especially when one considers that there is at least a quarter of employees who are actively disengaged in their work – they are only there for the money and for what they can get out of being there. This figure alone would be enough to stop even the toughest of business owners at the outset.

But despite all of the above, despite all of the complications and procedures and fallouts and wins, the absolute number one reason most businesses fail in this area of business building is the lack of capital in paying wages – they are astounded at the number of things that have to be included in paying staff. It's not just about paying a wage every week – and it's staggering how quickly pay day rolls around each time. It's about extras such as sick-leave entitlements, superannuation, holiday pay, insurances, mandatory staff training, penalty rates, OH&S costs.

No-one would argue that these costs are not well-deserved by employees (well for most of them), but what is the death blow to business is the unrelenting frequency with which they occur and the unstoppable onset of the need to pay out each and every week for your staff. And as stated above, the number one reason for business failures, is the lack of capital to keep things going. Time and time again the news proclaims the collapse of a business with workers demanding their final payouts and entitlements – and this happens to businesses on all ends of the spectrum. Again, cash flow is king. If you don't know about the intelligent way to use barter. And let's face it – not many even know about barter, let alone the best way to use it. So, for most business owners, relying on the incoming and outgoing of cash, contributes a great deal to their ultimate failure and huge losses. They are accustomed to thinking of cash flow in a limited way.

TRADE PRACTICES

For the new business owner, this area can be just as volatile an area as any of the others. And the rules change every day. Not only are there tax implications, restrictions, regulations and applications, there are also the industry specific parameters within which one is supposed to operate – the intricate and involved details of which the business owner is expected to be familiar with.

As stated elsewhere in this book, the recurring costs involved with keeping abreast of all the licensing, fees, certifications and so on can be daunting. But with the introduction of barter to a business there are some costs at least that can be defrayed with barter dollars.

For instance, the sometimes exorbitant costs that are incurred by using the services of an accountant can be offset by using an accountant who is part of the barter community. This way costs involved are paid in barter dollars and not cash dollars. The same is true for the services of lawyers and financial advisors.

MARKETING AND PROMOTION

The whole area of marketing can be as vast as the Sahara and just as unforgiving. Successful businesses often find the types of promotion and marketing that give the best results and stick to them. Mind you, it can take a few years, and barrels of lost cash before one is able to discover what it is that actually works best.

One of the most commonly cited bugbears for business owners, new and established is the exorbitant cost of marketing and advertising. It's like taking a daily dose of cod liver oil – you hate it, but in the long term you know it will be of benefit.

So it is with advertising – it has to be endured. If not for advertising how would your clients know where you are or what you do or how to buy from you? And it seems that every day there is a phone call from some advertiser offering a great deal and good incentives to have you advertise with them.

At first, many start-up business owners try anything that comes their way, erroneously believing that any form of advertising is good advertising. And within twelve months they have discovered to their horror that the thousands they have expended on advertising and marketing has brought in little cash flow. And once again, they realize that cash is king and they have been found wanting. The coffers are all but empty, but they have signed contracts with advertisers and newspapers and the television studios and they are required to pay thousands per month in costs.

Being able to use barter dollars in this area is a godsend to many businesses. Again, this means the saving of valuable cash reserves to enable the ongoing functioning of the business. What a huge boon this is!

STRATEGIZING WITH POLICIES AND PROCEDURES
One of the factors that are key to progressing a business and growing the bottom line, is the implementation of policies and strategies. Without them the business is just a mass of to-dos and checklists. The policies and strategies that are in place at the beginning can often mean the difference between the success and failure of a venture.

It's not the lure of being an administrative genius that brings thousands of would-be business operators to the starting line. In fact, this is where many beginners hire 'the wife' or friend or sister or someone's mother to 'do the books' and answer the phone. They are under the innocent and mistaken presumption that that this is all it takes to keep things going successfully. Usually the start-ups are not trained in business or the responsibilities involved in getting thing up and running. This is one of the reasons banks, councils, regulatory bodies and lending authorities often have some sort of business planning assistance available to beginners.

Implementing policies and strategies is not as simple as one might imagine. For instance, a restaurant strategy may require the installation of point of sale software that interfaces with the kitchen and maître d' station. The software and hardware required for this can be pricey and complicated, and sometimes, ongoing. If the business, no matter what it is, is able to find a supplier who uses barter then the whole system is simplified and cash flow is protected and able to be reserved for other facets of the business.

Without the use and development of the all important policies and strategies that are relevant to your particular industry, much of what you have worked for and anticipated could dissolve into nothing.

And yet many of the start-ups have materialized not because the new owner is savvy in business practice. Most times the start-up has occurred because the owner is a great process worker, or a great technician in their own right. They start out on their own, because they think they can do a better job of producing the product or service they have been expert in. The bigger picture doesn't often rate in the decision to start up on their own.

Employing consultants, buying expensive, industry specific software and hardware, keeping track of recent developments and trends can also have a major impact on the jolly cash king. The cash doesn't just materialize from nowhere. There are definite pluses and minuses that are involved and if there are too many minuses, then it doesn't take a genius to work out the long term future.

The policies and strategies that can be instituted in this way ensure that any business is able to continue to grow and improve. It is not held back by having to rely on cash flow or credit, at high rates, to continue its growth. This is an intelligent and forward thinking solution to the problem.

UP-KEEP AND RENOVATIONS

This is one of the areas in which barter comes into its own and it's also one of the areas in which businesses that don't use barter can suffer great losses. Anyone who has ever undertaken repairs, renovations, extensions, remodeling or fitting out of an office or business will know that when a quote is given, it is rarely the final price that is paid. Blow outs, delays, extensions to pricing, extras that weren't catered for and a whole range of things often conspire to inflate the final costs – so much so that sometimes a business is dealt a deadly blow before it is even able to open the doors! However, the brilliant joy of using barter in this regard is that it is possible to hire painters, plumbers, electricians, carpenters and all sorts using barter. If your networks are good and you have plenty of contractors in your area, then theoretically you won't have to pay out any cash for the hire of contractors.

Thousands of cash dollars can be preserved by using barter for renovations and the benefits don't end with contractor costs. The paint, the fixtures and fittings, the floor coverings, the office equipment, the computer systems, telecommunications systems and just about anything else you could think of are also available on barter.

It is possible to not only open a well presented and up-market entity to your customers, but it is possible to retain the cash that will be so desperately needed in other areas of the business. Savvy business owners have been using barter for decades to take their businesses to the next level without paying out big cash dollars.

There is a story about Cotton Joe – he knew he could produce better cotton than anyone else on the western seaboard. He had worked in the major factories and production plants for 15 years. He knew every aspect of the business, from purchasing the raw product, to cleaning, carding, spinning, weaving, bleaching and dyeing.

Every week for 10 years he had put aside some money – he had wanted to go out on his own for awhile. He had enough for a deposit on a small boutique domestic cotton factory that had come up for sale interstate. It was perfect. The bank lent him the rest of the money he needed, using his home as collateral, and he was away. He had never felt happier.

He knew he had to make some cosmetic changes to establish his own new brand, so the offices were refurbished, new paint colors were used around the factory, the car park had to be upgraded and of course, as the boss, he couldn't be seen driving around in his old pick-up. He bought a new 4x4. He wined and dined the right people and flew across the country demonstrating his new and improved product with organic, color-fast dyes and presented the blends that he had developed.

It was a thrilling time and all that he had ever hoped for seemed, at last, to be his for the taking. But then bills came in for the renovations and the updates. He had budgeted for $40,000 – and when the total came in at $95,000 he was immediately gripped with a fear that stopped him dead in his tracks. He had insisted on only the best for his new venture and only the best was provided. He had thought there would be a little extra to pay – but not this much, and now he couldn't be shamefaced and ask them to take the new things away. Then he discovered that the machinery in the factory was not in as good order as it was first claimed to be – there were major repairs that needed to happen before an upgrade in production could occur. So, he flew to more places to demonstrate his wares, he wined and dined more prospects and eventually spent his way into complete ruin.

Living and operating the business according to what one thinks it should be like, has often been the ruination of a perfectly good venture.

UTILITIES

Paying for utilities such as electricity, gas, water, rates and rubbish removal, can seem to be costs that should be easily paid. After all, they are easily absorbed by the incoming monies – aren't they? And yet, here again, the relentless regularity with which these costs are incurred can be the death knell for a struggling business. The extra costs, bonds, securities, upfront payments and demands that result from starting up in business can be unforeseen contingencies that cost dearly.

It would be wonderful to say that it was possible to pay for your utilities using barter as well. However, this is one area where, so far, it is not yet possible. These enterprises – electricity, gas, water and so on still require large cash injections on a regular basis and when one considers that the price of electricity is set to double over the next 10 years, it is comforting to know that cash flow will be there to cover the costs.

Now we are getting to the crux of why it is that some businesses seem to grow and thrive, no matter what the circumstances or the economic environment, whilst others sail down the gurgler with gusto.

There are systems and workings at play that assist some businesses beyond what is apparent at face value. And barter is definitely one of those systems.

AVOIDING THE LURE OF EASY CREDIT

For most of the first decade of the 21st century, there was nothing that was easier to come by than credit – on cars, houses, cards – whatever. It seemed that whatever we wanted we could have, and not just one house but several if we were savvy enough to make our credit work for us. But then the big bad credit crunch beamed down on the world and suddenly there wasn't money to be had for love nor money. Cities like Las Vegas, replete with millionaire playgrounds and mansions and more and more casino developments turned into a beggar's retreat almost overnight. The lost billions that seemed to vanish into nowhere suddenly tainted all borrowers with the same brush – greedy wannabes.

Businesses were not immune either – the easy credit they had used to fund expansions, takeovers, excessive CEO bonuses and salaries, suddenly dried up and of course, every day workers were the first to feel the full brunt of events. Redundancies, sackings, restructuring and downsizing were the flavor of the new times. For the first time since the 1930s in America, white collar workers were on the street, homeless, unemployed and desperate.

But in the way of things financial and the roller coaster rides many have become accustomed to, the talk nowadays is of full recovery and banks are beginning to up new advertisements promising great interest rates on loans and borrowings. The old ways are beginning to resurface as if they had never been gone and the cycle is set to run again. Only in the background do the wilderness criers call out for restraint, overhauling of systems and accountability, but they are soon denounced as nay sayers and left to cry out alone.

With no security, no other assets apart from the family home and no promise of guaranteed cash flow, businesses are again setting themselves up to be easy prey to the banks when and if things go wrong again.

Many businesses owners and operators feel that they are indeed at the mercy of the banks and lenders. They feel trapped by the constraints of their own circumstances. They know they are vulnerable and exposed. They also know that if they want their businesses to not only continue, but to thrive, they have to take financial risks to cover their outlays.

This is another major area where barter can prove to be very advantageous to the financial health of a business. In the long run, easy credit just means more repayments with more interest accruing and more indebtedness to the lending body. There is no quick fix to this spiral of dependency – and when things are going well, interest rates are low and all seems well, then no-one seems to complain much – they just keep drawing on more funds, or reducing their equity in their home. In the long term this can never result in a good thing, unless the business suddenly begins to bring in a whole lot more business than it has done before.

With the proper, effective and intelligent use of barter, it's not necessary to keep extending the reach of the loan's manager into your business. Barter allows for the exchange of goods and services where bags of cash are not needed. It's a very good alternative to securing more and more lines of credit that can never be repaid.

GOVERNMENT GRANTS AND ASSISTANCE

The governments of most developed countries realize the importance of the contributions made by business to the successful running of their societies. They realize too that the number of employees taken on by business, could be relying on government support and assistance without the presence of businesses and so it is in their best interests to give as much support to business as they can.

A quick perusal of any government business assistance website will provide you with a list of available resources and grants. But these are not for the faint hearted. These are for businesses that are strong in their success already and just need a bit more to take them to the next level. Most often these grants and subsidies are for businesses who turnover in excess of $50m – that's a lot to earn before you can get help. It's also one of the reasons you find governments helping to bail out some big industries, such as car manufacturers – because they have already invested a large amount of capital in the venture and don't want it all to be for naught.

For small businesses there are a few little packages available, but mostly help and advice lines, to assist in keeping things going in an organized manner. This is the area of highest risk and the government is not going to pour money down a lost cause.

Securing funding and support from government incentive schemes and grants is a good thing if you can get it – and it often ensures some pretty good advertising and support of your goods or services. Some schemes can pour millions of dollars into an enterprise or venture. However, these injections are fairly rare and you generally have to have a thriving business to begin with.

There are some funds that are available to start up businesses, and it would be a good idea to get on to as many of these as possible. Depending on the government of the day, it may be a worthwhile exercise.

Barter is of no relevance here except to allow you to hang on to the cash reserves you have been granted. It means that you don't have to spend your cash dollars on everything that you need.

LIVING THE DREAM

So why do business owners bother? Why do they do this to themselves? Why do they go out onto the very edge thinking that their business will be different, that they will be able to survive where thousands of others have failed?

More than any other reason provided is this one. They want to be the boss. They want to be the one who calls the shots, who comes and goes as they please and who makes the important decisions. They want the freedom of lifestyle they imagine comes from owning your own business.

Take Ellery for example. Ellery was a production line kitchen flat pack worker. Every day he cut out the templates for someone else's new kitchen. Every day he watched as the fat cats in the office sat around big noting themselves. Every day he knew he could the same as them, only better. Then one day his chance came – his wife received a nice public service redundancy package and they both agreed to take the plunge.

Pretty soon Ellery was in new premises with all the new equipment he needed, with the appropriate bank loans, vehicle leases, office fit out and the rest of the kit and caboodle. Now he was the boss, he would be able to create the lifestyle he had so longed for.

For a short time they had enough work to keep them going and they were doing okay. But then the orders weren't coming in as frequently – the whole country was talking recession and gloom and doom. He realized that his timing could have been better. People were putting off getting the new kitchen and they were also putting off buying that new home they were after.

Before long, Ellery was a production line kitchen flat pack worker. He had lost the lot, managed to save the house, but now had massive loans he had to repay to get over his foray into the business world. Only now, Ellery didn't even look up when the 'fat cats' were around. He didn't want to go there again.

There are thousands of Ellerys that start up against all odds hoping to fulfill their dream of living the good life and being the boss. In reality, it's a whole lot different and if you're not well prepared or experienced, then the shock of reality can be enough to tip one over the edge. Personal stress and hardship counseling as a result of business failure is a common occurrence, and becoming more so.

So why do we do it? Because there is a buzz that results from striving to get things up and running and seeing customers pay for your goods and services, and there is that thrill of knowing you have created something that is valued by others. There is also the freedom of being responsible only to yourself (this is a double edged sword), and there is the ever present dream of knowing it can only get better. This is the essence of why people take inordinate risks to go into business. This is why they risk so much.

We talked about the way in which some business owners set about sabotaging their own efforts by giving in to the pressures of 'image' and 'branding'. They overspend, don't allow for extra inclusions in quotes and end up being at the mercy of blown out budgets and creditors.

There's no doubt that image and branding are an important aspect of doing business. No-one likes to think they are entering into a financial relationship with a business that can't even afford a can of paint or decent office. But image consultants, designers, office fit-outs, vehicles ... are all available on barter. There is really no need to go into debt to cover the costs of good presentation. It is possible with barter to live the good life and keep your cash too. This is one of the reasons why some businesses just seem to keep on improving and others go to the wall.

With barter, you can go on that holiday, drive that car, hire that consultant and entertain at fancy restaurants. You can live the dream – guilt free, stress free and still hold on to your cash reserves for the important payments such as wages, utilities, rent and the like.

BETTING THE HOUSE

Depending on your lending body, and the measures they have in place to secure their loans, it is not surprising that they usually insist on having the family home, or some other sizeable asset, as part or all of the collateral on a business loan. Sometimes they will even include, cars, chattels, fixtures and fittings as part of the arrangement. This means that should thing ultimately go wrong, and the business fails, as they do in over 80% of cases, then the bank has access to everything you own, in order to make good on their loan – oh, and then of course, you will usually have been forced to take out mortgage insurance as well, which is another body that has entitlement to your possessions.

The other side of this coin is that the bank is generally reticent to give business loans unless they are presented with a very good business plan and/or model. However, this also depends on factors such as the amount of equity in the home, the income of other members of the household and the current state of the economy and interest rates. During times of boom, banks are more than easy to convince to part with their funds for any reasonable purpose. However, when things go wrong and there are sudden downturns, they can be the last ones who will be eager to help you out – unless you have more equity, more ability to repay and so on.

And so it is that when people are still in the euphoric stage of starting a business and flying on the wings of the dream and the adrenalin of the vision, they can tend to overlook the fine print and the inherent warnings that come with getting in too deep with the banks or any other lending body.

'But it will never come to that!' is the phrase that ticks along in the back of the new start business owner's mind. 'My business is different. I know more about business than they think I do. I have a better product and selling at a good profit is not going to be a problem.' The many instances of self-talk convince them to go ahead and make it all happen, after all, no pain no glory. And one thing that can be said of the human spirit, it is adventurous and courageous and enamored of the thrill of winning. It will keep trying in the face of obvious defeat and it will resurrect itself in the most trying of circumstances until crying 'uncle' is the only option left.

Then follows the shame of defeat – with the recriminations and the re-possessions of the house, the chattels, the car and your dignity. Usually it's not until this happens that the blinkers are removed and the vision of what was once a golden opportunity is now seen as a decayed and tangled rotting mess.

How many business owners wake in the middle of the night with the shakes and night terrors, gripped with dread and foreboding. There are some who just continue on, making suppliers and anyone else they can think of, wait for their payments, sometimes for months, even years. There are others who just don't want to know and will pretend that it will all change soon enough, when the economy picks up, when the tourist season gets here, when the rain stops, when the new accountant gets things together, when the new leads eventuate.

Then there are others still whose new best friend is their loans manager and easy credit lines mean less pressure, no more hassle and more opportunities to live the good life. If there's a problem, just get another loan, that's what it's all about right? And in the good times this is what happened to too many businesses and the banks for their part were very quick to extend more loans instead of closing an account. To them it made better sense to keep increasing the possibility of repayments and keeping their customers locked in for longer periods of time with complicated banking products and the like. It was all a great ride and no-one seemed to be complaining, until the banks themselves went bust and started calling in loans from where ever they could.

Take Terry for instance – he is just one example of a guy who thought that his business would be the next best thing. He did all of the above without barter and ended up losing the lot, including the house and the car. Terry's family were furious that he should have made them so financially vulnerable by including the family home as collateral against the bank loan.

Now, he likes his caravan, although it's not paid for yet, still renting it and some of the people in the van park are okay on a good day – but most of the time Terry just sits and thinks about all that he has lost and how vain and inglorious his actions had been. If he had his time over he would stay away from the 'thrill' of opening his own business and be happy with his lot. But too late for that now.

Terry is just one of thousands who lose it all. But if you're not planning to join him anytime soon, then think about the intelligent alternative of using barter as a part of your business plan. It is the sensible, rational and savvy thing to do.

While you may still have to collateralize your home to obtain your bank loans, but you will have organized things so that you will always have enough cash on hand to service the loans. The wolf will happily be kept from the door.

DESPERATE MEASURES

Operating from a place of desperation always leads to more problems. Decisions are made in haste and with feelings of fear and lack always heightened at the fore front. It is virtually impossible to make clear, objective and rational decisions from a place of desperation.

In fact, how is it possible to think clearly when one is always reeling from the shock of night terrors and living in dread of the telephone and mail box? And yet so many choose to live this way rather than using the options that were available.

There are several sayings that come to mind once things have gone sour.

- Desperate times demand desperate measures.
- Waiting for the axe to fall.
- When you're backed into a corner, come out fighting.
- Keeping the wolf from the door.
- The odds are stacked against you.

All of them can be applicable and all of them can be used as excuses, but one thing remains, the failed business owners who were once so full of enthusiasm and hope have most often been destroyed by their own dream and find it very difficult to recover from the defeat.

And yet there are those incessantly good humored, optimistic and well grounded business owners, who will write off a loss, re-group, get themselves in order and keep marching on to bigger and better things. These are the ones who will usually succeed in the long run. They learn from their mistakes and take good advice on board. Their next venture is never as exposed or risky as the last. That is to say, these business owners are the ones who have a philosophical outlook that sustains them during the tough times.

There are others though, who will resort to any desperate measure they see available, just to get them out of the bind. These people unfortunately, are the ones who give business a bad name. They are the ones who up and leave in the middle of the night. They are the ones who leave a long line of broken promises and shattered contractual agreements. These are also the ones who break people's spirits, promise things they can't deliver and often move on to wreak havoc in someone else's neighborhood.

Anyone who has ever found themselves in a desperate financial struggle can empathize with those who react out of fear and dread, but there are those who choose ethics and character over knee-jerk reactions and over-reactions.

For many, even in strained circumstances, it is still not too late. It may still be possible to resurrect the business with the injection of barter dollars. It is possible for some to slowly bring themselves back from the brink with the use of barter. Use barter dollars for as much as is possible and reserve the cash flow or use it as necessary and see the business start to turn around.

The wolf at the door, can be tamed and lured away.

CHAPTER THREE

SUMMARY

- Barter is system by which businesses exchange goods and services without the use of money.

- Preserving cash flow for important purposes will help to keep a business afloat during tough times.

- Over 80% of new start-up businesses fail in the first five years.

- Preserving cash flow for important purposes will help to keep a business afloat during tough times.

- The sensible rules of barter use make it an equitable system for all businesses.

- Those who succeed are the ones who have enough capital to sustain them fully for at least a year.

- Cash flow is king.

- Credit that is easy is easily overwhelming.

- It is possible to live the dream if barter and cash can be combined.

- Some of the extreme circumstances in which businesses find themselves can be avoided or offset if barter had been introduced.

CHAPTER FOUR

CHOOSING YOUR OWN MARKET SUCCESS

There are a lot of things that go into creating success.
I don't like to do just the things I like to do. I like to do
things that cause the company to succeed. I don't spend a
lot of time doing my favorite activities

—Michael Dell

BEING DETERMINED TO SUCCEED

Michael Dell, Bill Gates, Anita Roddick – all hugely successful business owners and managers and all began with the notion that their ventures **would be** successful. For them there was no choice. Failure was not option, and while there are hundreds of thousands of startups that begin with the same notion, it is usually a vain hope rather than a certain destiny that inspires them to begin in the first place.

Michael Dell is serious when he says 'I like to do things that cause the company to succeed.' Most business owners come at the dream of running a hugely successful business from the premise that it will be a quick and sure fire way to granting them the eternally blissful lifestyle they have been searching for. They take time away. They play. They go on holiday. There are long 'networking' lunches and the list goes on. In the meantime the business is supposed to be growing and bringing in money – somehow, someway, somewhere. But with no captain at the helm, it is easy for the business to lose its focus and direction and be drifting aimlessly in the fog.

A *successful* business owner is committed to his or her own success. It's about a commitment. When you commit to your life partner, for better or for worse, in sickness and in health, 'til death do you part – that's a pretty serious promise you make to someone. These days of course every second couple doesn't last the distance and one wonders about the commitment, and if it was there in the first place. A good, strong, steady and successful relationship is not all a bed of roses. Just ask anyone who's been in a relationship longer than five years.

There are times when any relationship is challenged. There are times when the slamming of a door and the packing of a bag are only prevented by the smallest of things. There are times when making up is the hardest thing you've ever had to do. And then there are times when it doesn't just involve the two of you anymore – there are other precious lives that are affected by poor decisions and angry words. Then there are the expectations and pressures that are put on a relationship by society – firstly there are the expectations you have of each other, and then the expectations put upon couples by the extended family mix. And finally there are the expectations from friends and society at large. There is the gender card and role expectation. There is a huge amount of pressure.

It is no secret that a good and strong marriage requires commitment. Before all and sundry you have made an out loud promise to commit to this relationship, to do the absolute best that you can do to keep it together. That's a tall order – and it really is no surprise that many marriages fail.

That's likewise why it really is no surprise that many businesses fail. Sometimes that commitment to succeed is more than the business owner can bear. Sometimes that commitment to succeed is just not strong enough to keep it all together.

So, before you read on, before you decide what you're going to do to work on your business to take it to the next level, before you do any of the planning for success – decide in your own heart that this is absolutely, truly *the* thing you want for yourself. And then commit to it. Promise yourself that you will not stop until you have succeeded. At the grass roots level, that is the most basic of steps to gaining a successful business. Take a few minutes in a quiet space and time to evaluate the commitment you have made to your business. Is there room for improvement? Is the commitment as robust as you would have it be? What changes do you need to make to it? And more than just being committed to succeed are you committed to doing things the intelligent way? Most of the very successful companies like Dell, The Body Shop, Microsoft, Xerox – succeeded because they had a vision of doing things that were different.

Using and applying barter to your system of operations is probably one of the most intelligent ways of centering your vision and focus. From the start, your stresses and fears are somewhat allayed because you know there is not as much pressure on the cash dollar as there is in other businesses. Using barter from the start is a great way to get a head start in your own business. It takes the worry out of the startup. It is a different way to go. It is the secret currency that has been used for thousands of years. It has often been the reason behind why one business fails miserably and another flourishes.

COMMITTING TO SUCCESS
What is in a name?

Once you have absolutely committed yourself and your business to success, there are a number of things you can do which will arguably give you a significant edge over your competitors, the least of which is the choice of your business name.

If a customer has to think hard about what your business does and is not informed of this by your business name, then chances are you are losing out on market presence and visibility. For instance, think about the difference in these two titles – Kwik Kopy versus Fast Service – Kwik Kopy tells it like it is. Immediately you know you will receive photocopying or printing services – quickly! Fast Service is also a quick copy company but from the name of the business you would never know it. They languish at the bottom of the market because no-one knows or recognizes quickly, what it is that they actually do. So, when you're looking to get some printing done quickly, who are you going to call?

Names are important. Think carefully about the names you give to your products and services. If there is no perceived value in the name, there will be no perceived value to the customer either. And if you're no good a thinking of a name, then consult a professional from the barter network and get some branding ideas too.

Business persona

'Oh don't go to them. They treat you like you don't exist. They always mix up orders and there is never any follow-up to see if you're happy with the product. Emil over the road is much better. He charges more, but it's so worth it.'

How many times have you heard comments similar to these? How many times have you said them yourself? The reality is, people like to be treated well. We all know that. We all like to feel that way ourselves. We all know that customer service is paramount, but how many times do we put our less than best foot forward and still expect our customers to keep coming back for more? It's an inane absurdity!

Your reputation in business is priceless. And it is one of the easiest things to destroy. We all start off with the best intentions – to have a sparkling, shiny operation that is flawless and ultra-successful, but reality often gets in the way. The storeman didn't receive the orders in the correct way, and that has put out the stock operator and now pricing has become confused and then there was the flu that knocked out six of your staff for a week, and then there was school holidays and then there was the storm ... and ... and ... and ultimately you never seem to be able to get on top of things. The last thing you have time to think about is the customer. You end up getting annoyed at the very person or business that is bringing in your money. This is business suicide.

Developing and instituting appropriate systems to organize and prevent the fallout from the above, is the only way to ensure continued improvement, business growth and success. If you and your systems are letting your business down – fix them immediately. And if you can't afford to fix them – again, USE THE BARTER NETWORK. Get it done before all the thrills and spills of each business day, ruin your future forever.

Creating customer loyalty

Gianni and Reba had the best Italian restaurant in town. For 15 years it was the number one destination in the town for parties, birthdays, Valentine's, wakes, dinners and memories. The second generation of loyal and devoted customers was being weaned on their pastas and pizzas and it was all very happily ever after stuff. But then the big bad wolf came along in the form of another restaurant on the same block. It was a steak house.

When they heard about it, Gianni and Reba laughed off the possible threat to their business by saying: 'Our customers have been with us for 15 years! They won't leave us for that showy flash in the pan!'

They dismissed the drop in bookings in the first couple of weeks as seasonal and due to the snow storms that had come in from the north. They dismissed next month's drop in takings as the result of increased interest rates and higher petrol prices – people had less disposable income to spend on eating out. By the time six months had passed, they were having to re-think their viability for next year. For the first time in 15 years, there was the possibility that they may not be open in the summer for the tourist trade. They were devastated by the thought of faithful, loyal customers being drawn away from them. How could this be? These were more than customers, these were their friends now surely!

In business today, the sad truth is, there is no such thing as a loyal customer. Maybe it was the case years ago, but not anymore. With the pressures on everyone's budget, the best deal that comes along is the one that attracts the customers, for this time at least. That is not to say that businesses have to compete by price – the old saying of live by the sword, die by the sword is truer here than anywhere. If you live by cost cutting you will die by cost cutting.

Only 5% of customers shop by price alone. And that leaves 95% who are looking for more than a dollar value in their purchase. For instance if you want to buy a set of knives and find a set at Joe's Bargain Basement for $15, you may be tempted. But at $15 you know that they probably won't last long, may lose their edge and their handles won't take the caustic nature of dishwashers. So, you know from the start that the $15 set probably isn't a good choice. However, at Staysharp you can buy a similar set for around $35. This product is guaranteed quality and added to the purchase price is the promise of a free lifelong sharpening service and a protective sheath in which to store the knives. Added to that, you have the joy of being served by professionals who take pride in what they do and in how they do business. You are treated as royalty and always enjoy going in to browse their new items as they arrive. You also appreciate the knowledge they have of their product, such as the advantages you will gain by using tungsten blades as opposed to stainless steel and so on.

Staysharp has added value to your purchase all along the way. They have treated you as you wish to be treated and they have made provision for the future by giving you lifelong sharpening services. This is how customer loyalty is won. What business owners fail to realize is that customer loyalty is not about the customer being loyal to your business, it's about you being loyal to your customers and giving them the best value for their choices.

If you want to increase revenue instantly, one of the best ways of doing this is to triple the *perceived* value of your product today. This doesn't always have to include price reduction – in fact raising your prices rather than reducing them, whilst adding exceptional value is the best way to go about promoting customer loyalty. When you consider that the actual price for making a Dolce & Gabbana handbag is probably around $20 and the sale price can be around US$1,171, and buyers are flocking to the site to purchase them, then price is not the issue here. It doesn't have to be so for your business either.

Add value by increasing the level of service – that costs you nothing but gives your customer plenty. Add guarantees, extra services, free gifts, VIP notification to events etcetera. This list is limitless.

It is six times easier to sell to your existing customers than it is to attract new customers. It will also cost you a good deal less in advertising and marketing. Customers never consider making a purchase from the viewpoint of 'what can I do for my business owner?' It's always from the viewpoint of 'what can this business do for me and my needs?' and if you can answer that question successfully, you will be developing a loyal customer base – at least for as long as you maintain your high standards.

The next time you go to a café or restaurant and are greeted by the laconic Gen Y who doesn't really care what you want or how you get it, stop for a moment and consider how much that business is losing in return customer sales.

MANAGING CASH FLOW

After commitment, the next most important thing to consider is your cash flow. After all without it, there is no business there is only a hobby that you are supporting or a mountain of debt that you are creating. There are zillions of words that have been written about cash flow. And most of them have been ignored, because many business owners erroneously, arrogantly, foolishly think that they know about money and how it works. And they are good with money aren't they? Are they? Outlined below are some quick and useful hints and tips on how to amalgamate your best business methods with barter.

Control the expenses

You should know what things cost. You should know what the average price for supplies, product and delivery are. If you don't know then you should find out from your industry trade associations or advisors. If you are paying too much, change it. If you are paying for a three pronged approach – such as paying the grower, the supplier and the manufacturer, then find a way to simplify the process to your best advantage.

Always know your categories of expenses and keep a firm hold on them. It's easy for costs to board that runaway train and never be slowed again. Things such as ensuring that employees always use cost effective methods of doing things and not opting for the expensive methods just because they are easier – such as using operator assisted calls when needing a phone number, instead of using the free directory number. It all adds up.

A wealthy man knows where he spends every cent. He knows what's going out and what's coming in. He knows the difference in prices due to seasonal fluctuations, currency markets, wages blowouts and every other tiny little thing that impacts their product and sales. He knows too that using any legal method that helps offset cash flow is a good thing.

Increase sales

Many a business has apparently gone from struggling or ordinary to highly successful by finding that one deal, that one product, that one exceptional service that has blown the lid off the market and sent purchasers scurrying to buy, buy, buy. To the casual onlooker this may seem to be the result of some very good luck, but to the astute observer or fellow business owner, it will appear to be exactly what it is – the result of hard work, experimentation, change, loss, defeat, renewal, adjustment and a whole lot of tweaking.

Maintaining a commitment to succeed, the commitment to winning and combining that with the continued efforts will eventually result in a great product that people are lining up for. It is possible. it happens every day.

Using barter

So far this book has mentioned many and various ways in which barter could be used for your business. There are many more ways still in which you can control and conserve cash flow. Arguably the best way to do this is not to spend your cash at all – except for the necessities. But how does a business owner manage to do this? One such way is to max out the potential in your barter line as a rule of thumb before turning to cash.

At a quick glance, here are just some of the categories in which you can use barter:

Abrasives & adhesives

Accommodation

Advertising & marketing

Agriculture & farm services

Air conditioning & ventilation

Aircraft & airport services

Alcoholic beverages & services

Antiques, memorabilia & medals

Appliances & Heating

Art, craft & hobbies

Art galleries & museums

Asphalt services

Audio & visual services

Automation systems

Automotive services

Baby & children services

Bags, handbags & luggage

Bathroom & kitchen services

Battery sales & service

Beauty services

Boat & marine services

Building & construction

Business, financial & legal services

Caravan, campervan & motorhome services

Catering services

Cleaning & hygiene

Clothing & accessories

Communications

Computer/internet product & services

Curtains, blinds, awnings & shutters

Dental services

Diesel services

Doors, gates & fencing

Dry-cleaning, laundry & ironing

Earthworks

Electrical

Engineering

Entertainment

Fiberglass services

Fitness services

Flooring

Florist & florist supplies

Food & drink services

Forklifts, trolleys & hand trucks

Function venues

Furniture

Garden nursery products & services

Glass mirrors & windows

Hardware

Health services

Hire equipment

Holidays & activities

Home décor, homewares & gifts

Home entertainment equipment

Home improvements & maintenance

Horse industry

Human resources services

Hydraulics & hose services

Ice & cool room services

Insulation services

Interior decorators & services

Jewellers

Leather clothing & leather goods

Lighting & accessories

Limousines & driver services

Machinery, tools & compressors

Manufacturers & fabricators

Medical and pharmaceutical
    services

Metal products & services

Multi-media services

Music

Office services

Optical services

Packaging materials & service

Painting & powder coating

Paper plastic & rubber products

Pet & animal services

Photographic product & services

Plumbing & drainage

Printing & design services

Property agents, valuers &
    auctioneers

Pump product & services

Refrigeration services

Secondhand dealers

Security, fire & safety services

Sharpening service

Shops & markets

Signs & signwriters

Sporting & camping

Sporting clubs

Stationery, books & magazines

Stone products & services

Storage & transport services

Surveyor services

Swimming pools spas & saunas

Telephone equipment & services

Textiles & haberdashery

Tours

Training & tuition

Upholsterers & canvas products

Vending machines

Wedding services

Wood, timber & saws

Wool, feather & down products

As you can see, it's rather an exhaustive list. And if there isn't something here that you can use as part of your business expenses, then you must be a rare gem indeed. As has been mentioned before, the best way to make barter work for your business is to put as many business expenses on your barter dollar use rather than cash use.

When you are intelligently and systematically combining barter and cash flow, then there *must* be an improvement in the cash flow situation. And rather than scrambling at every turn to meet the regular payments and outgoings for the business, you will find that there is always enough there to make it happen. Your road to success has to be easier. And if there is still not enough cash to cover expenses, then you have some serious problems in your business that need immediate attention.

ACHIEVING PEAK PRODUCTIVITY
In this fast paced, results driven business environment of the western world, it really is the quick or the dead. The highest energy wins, according to some leading lights in the business sector. There's no time to spend weighing up twenty or thirty options. There's no time to lose in developing that new product, tweaking that marketing headline, in training staff to upsell, in delving into potential profit areas for the future. It should all be happening now. The results should be pouring in now. The ramifications should be felt now. The plans should be coming to fruition now.

Too many businesses operate like start ups for years and never move on to the next stage of their development. The owners then sit back and bemoan their lot to whoever will listen. When there are no plans for success, no moves towards improvement, no systems analysis or placement, no P&L statements studied on a regular basis, when none of these things is happening then failure is a certainty. The old adage of 'fail to plan and you plan to fail' has never been truer.

A business that is set to bring in a sizeable return, is more than just a hobby with a few expenses attached – or at least it should be. And just as in any venture worth its salt, you reap what you have sown. You can't expect to have a silk purse when all you've managed to create is a sow's ear of things.

Time management

But it's not all gloom and doom, even when you have made a mess of things. We are all allowed our mistakes in life and we are all allowed an epiphany to get us out of the quagmire. This means that while you have made mistakes, you are allowed to move beyond them. Too many business owners find that once they have taken refuge under the umbrella of 'poor struggling workaholic' they never need to emerge in any other form. They spend years under this cloud, without realizing that with some very small effort they could shed the limitations and move on to a new reputable umbrella of 'highly successful business man/woman.'

And the best way to make big changes quickly? Manage your time better. There are whole industries devoted to this seemingly ethereal quest. But as in a lot of areas, it is common sense that brings the best results. Too many bosses, business owners, operate under the misguided notion that they are indispensable and that they have to be present to manage every crisis, no matter how big or small. They feel they have to be available to suppliers, customers, friends, the delivery man and anyone else who may decide to drop in. It's no wonder that they then have to burn the midnight oil in the vain attempt to get the things done that should have been done during the working day.

They do this sort of merry-go-round cum bumper-ride day in and day out. It never seems to end. They become increasingly frustrated and find that no matter how hard they try, they never seem to be getting beyond the basics – moving the business to the next level! You must be joking. Just making it to the end of the week without going broke and keeping things ticking along is the best they can hope for.

So, what would happen if you refused to take calls, answer mobiles, respond to emails, texts, voice messages or snail mail? What would happen if you only relegated a certain time of the day to these practices? Would your business cease to exist? Probably not. The reception staff would have to do their work and get on with answering the regular queries and so on, and clients, customers, suppliers and all the rest would soon come to know that you are an important, busy person getting on with work – getting on with actually running your business.

What would happen if you stopped listening to every petty staff concern and comment that arose. What if you stopped listening to the mundane tedium that didn't concern you at all. What if you stopped trying to solve everyone's problems, especially when there are perfectly well trained staff available to do what you are doing? What would happen really? Perhaps the wheels would fall off for an hour or two, but more often than not, what tends to happen is that people rise to the occasion. They develop the pride that comes with being a part of a team that excels and takes responsibility for itself.

What is extraordinarily amazing is the number of business owners who believe that having systems and practices in place is only for the ostentatious, anally retentive stalwarts of yesteryear. Nothing could be further from the truth. Truly successful businesses always, always, always have rigorous systems and policies in place to ensure their success. And time management is where they start first.

Several studies into this area have been made, the most interesting of which concurred that only about 10% of the work day is spent on income producing activity. The rest of the day is taken up with minutia and unnecessary distraction. That's an appalling result – and one that is totally unacceptable for anyone wanting to grow a successful business. If you're happy to continue in an unremarkable journey with below-par results, then keep doing what you're doing. But when you're ready to realize the best results possible, then start taking charge, especially of those time-consuming, non-productive interruptions that eat into your work day and ultimately your profit margins.

FOCUSING AND GOAL SETTING

This is another key area that can seriously detract from your status as a serious business concern in the real world. Too many times a business remains small in mindset, small in results and small in possibilities because there is no real focusing of effort or direction.

Keeping your eye on the ball, so to speak is the only way to keep your intentions and results on the right path. You must focus your attention and energies into producing those results you have been planning for. Without this kind of focus, your business turns into a veritable treadmill – always moving, always expending energy, but never getting anywhere. Your business is worth more than that and your efforts deserve greater returns than that.

If you have gone to the great trouble of producing a business plan, then make sure you use it. Hone it, develop it, amend it and keep focusing on the end goals.

There has been much talk and hoo-ha about goals and goal setting and finishing what you have started and the like, until many businesses are just worn out just by thinking about the process, let alone doing anything about it. But it doesn't have to be that way.

Most businesses are born out of the thrill and excitement of what could be and how it will all end up – setting goals and objectives in order to achieve those ends should be just as thrilling. It's like setting out stepping stones across the river to get to the proverbial other side. It's great stuff. It's about possibilities and energies and strategies and using all the skills one has to best plot the path.

Too many times, business owners look at the idea of goal setting as a mundane, boring, inappropriate waste of time. They know in their heads where they want to go and how they want to go about it, and to them that should be enough. They'll tell staff only what they need to know and it should all just go along smoothly till the end game is won.

In theory that sounds fine, but the reality is, that it rarely works that way. Staff are often confused, unallied, disparate and disengaged from the processes and the end game results. They feel they have no course to follow and are totally reliant on the pearls of wisdom that emanate from their fearless leader.

It doesn't take an expert to realize that staff always work best when they have outlined policies and procedures – yes those dirty words, policy and procedure and systems, all hated by the new wave of business owners because they are often perceived as the stodgy way to get things done, these are the real ways to keep focused and goal oriented.

This does not mean to say that once a goal is set, it is set in stone – on the contrary, the great goals of great business are almost always regularly updated and amended. There is a continual tweaking and refining. To have spent weeks or months coming up with desired goals, policies, procedures and systems and then to abandon them to the holy tablets that are only revered and never touched, is true folly.

The road map, the plan, the way ahead, all of those clichéd terms for getting things moving in the right direction, all of them, rely on what you have set out to be your focus. Losing sight of the focus and the goals can spell disaster for any business.

Importance of timelines

What never ceases to amaze me is the lack of importance many struggling, and even well-established businesses seem to place on time lines. And by time lines we mean putting a time and a date on all expectations and goals.

It's one thing to say, in November we will expect sales figures to increase by 25%. And then when you're meeting in December to discuss last month's P&Ls and there was a decline in sales rather than the increase you had hoped for, managers and bosses and workers alike, can throw their arms in the air, declare there is no use to all this planning, and it's all market driven and let's just get on with producing product. And so there are no more predictions or goal setting, or serious planning apart from accommodating events and meetings as they crop up.

From the receptionist, the bookkeeper and the process worker, to middle and upper management, there should be serious commitment made to the mindset of the timeline.

Instead of agreeing with a supplier that you should meet sometime soon to discuss next year's projected costs, you, or whomever it is that speaks with the supplier should respond in terms such as 'It would be great to meet with you to discuss these things. How does next Friday at two o'clock sound? We could discuss trends, the new players in the game and some of the plans I have in mind for product development.'

Having a direct and planned approach to meeting up not only saves a lot of wasted time in appointment making and the like, but it also sets an agenda for the meeting so there is less wasted time. When you become accustomed to thinking this way, you will be amazed at the difference it makes to how you are perceived. People will come to regard you as a person who should be taken seriously and one who knows what they want and how to go about getting it. You will also be amazed at quickly the results begin to show in your bottom line.

Timelines should also be applied to the goals you have set. For instance, if you're planning a 25% increase in sales for November – plan, week by week, day by day, exactly how you will go about achieving this. And stick to the schedules you have given yourself. You will soon discover whether you have been too ambitious or not. And rather than throwing up your arms in horror and despair, you will be able to adjust and tweak for more increased sales next month.

CHAPTER FOUR

SUMMARY

- Being a success is a matter of mindset.

- A strong business name can bring in interest and sales on its own merit.

- Building a strong and reliable business reputation is worth its weight in gold.

- Customer loyalty is what you make it – if you are loyal to your customers, they will return the favor.

- Cash flow combined with the intelligent use of barter can hugely increase cash flow.

- Peak productivity is the result of planning and time management.

- If you fail to plan, you plan to fail.

CHAPTER FIVE

FIND A MENTOR

Never give in ... never, never, never, in nothing great or small, large or petty, never give in except to convictions of honour and good sense. Never yield to force ... never yield to the apparently overwhelming might of the enemy.
—Winston Churchill

WHAT IS A MENTOR?

In general terms, when we refer to a mentor we refer to a teacher, a guide, an experienced person who is training an inexperienced person. Traditionally a mentor was a type of advisor to the young, but these days whole commercial sectors are based on mentoring, coaching and supporting business owners and companies. A myriad of information, courses, training manuals, boot camps and the like have been devised to re-shape and re-train our thinking and the way we do business.

A mentor these days is someone or a group of people to whom a business owner is able to turn to get advice and receive training in all things business – or specialized areas, if that is what is required. For instance if you feel your business Is lacking direction in marketing, then you could have a marketing mentor who will direct your marketing activities in the best way they see fit. You can either take the advice and implement it or not – it depends on how successful you want your business to be.

It should be stated here that for the most part, mentors tend to be interested parties in your business who may or may not have a vested interest in its success. Usually a mentor is a successful person in an industry like yours and one with whom you have a good relationship. It's a bit like the uncle taking the nephew under his wing and advising him about the best ways to get ahead – assuming of course, that the uncle is already successful and the nephew wants the advice the uncle is giving. Taking advantage of experience and knowledge is a good thing.

WHY WE NEED A MENTOR

There are some single minded business owners out there who are determined to re-invent the wheel, break their backs inventing systems that have been invented and improved already and basically make their own lives, and that of their families, a misery – just so long as they are left alone and feel they owe nothing to anyone. This is well and good, for someone who lives in a cave with nothing else to do in life except be miserable and enjoy suffering – goodness knows the world always has room for another martyr. Probably the most unexpected thing that this type of business owner would recognize is that s/he doesn't have to make it that hard – they don't have to be a slave to the fundamentals of their business and remain bogged down in the quagmire of minutiae and systems. We are well into the 21st century and well versed with the internet – there are literally millions of sites freely giving information and advice and supplying excellent material.

So, why do we need a mentor? We need one if we want to get ahead before we reach the age of retirement – we need one if we want to keep up with all that is happening in our industry. We need one if we want to de-stress and discuss things with someone who understands the ins and outs of those things that are distressing us. We need one if we don't want to get discouraged and fall down before the finish line. We need one if we want to keep energized and inspired. All of the most able and successful business owners have them – in whatever form that may be. And more than anything we need one if we don't want to waste a ton of time making the same mistakes others have made in the past.

WHAT TO LOOK FOR IN A MENTOR

Sometimes there are those who would have us believe that for a sum of money they will provide us with all we need to know about being successful – some of these may be charlatans and some may not. Some may wish to take advantage and others are only out to pass on valuable information because they care enough about their industry and their society to know that it's prudent to give someone a helping hand, and more often than not, they have been in receipt of the occasional helping hand themselves. So how do you tell the difference? How do you know whose advice is the best and whose should be disregarded? In short, the only way to answer these questions is to think of it in the following terms.

If you want to learn about how to change a tire for instance, you can ask several mentors. They may tell you about the best tire iron to use, the best tires to have to avoid the flat in the first place, and they may tell you the best way to release the rim, undo the nuts and advise you about the best place to put the jack. You may ask a dozen mentors the same questions and you will probably get a dozen different answers – you are the only one who will be able to decide which advice best fits your particular circumstance. You may decide to go with the advice from someone who has the same type of car, same type of tire and the same jack and tire iron – this will give you the best possible advice in the long run, because the variables in your situations are the same. You will soon come to know which information is relevant to you and which is not.

This leads us to the following important point – you will work best with the mentor whose character, style, results, industry and methods are most like the ones you want to emulate or develop. If you want to be the best then have the best as a mentor – choose the mentor or person you admire most and think the way they think, do the things they do, follow the same leads they do, mix with the same people they do. In short, there are five things to look for in a good mentor:

1 Knowledge
2 Work ethic
3 Business success
4 Influence
5 Future outlook

Knowledge

One of the most important reasons you have for choosing a mentor is to increase your industry knowledge and business operations techniques in as short a time as possible – so you are not going to choose a mentor who knows less about doing business in your industry than you do. It is just common sense.

Take a few minutes and think about your industry – who are the shining lights in that industry? Who is famous in that industry as being a brilliant business owner and developer in the industry? Whom do you immediately think of? Who is it that you would want to be like? Whose success do you want to emulate? This is the person to have as your mentor. If you already know this person and have a working relationship with them, then invite them to dinner, get to know them some more, ask if they would be interested in mentoring you. Ask about some of the problems you have been facing. Ask if they have some suggestions. Ask. Ask. Ask.

If it is not possible, or they are not willing, or are unable, or you are not in a position to be able to meet with them personally then make them your invisible mentor. Read all that they have written about the industry. Read and research the articles they have been quoted in. Find forums or chat rooms on the internet where their work is being discussed. Seek out anything that you can that will give you some insights about their success and how they attained it. And then, refer back to these basics and information pieces regularly – you will be amazed at the new information that comes forth on each reading.

Work ethic

It is very rare to find a successful business owner who has arrived at their success without inputting a lot of hours and a lot of hard work. Thomas Jefferson seemed to get it right when he said: 'I'm a great believer in luck, and I find the harder I work, the more I have of it.' So many times we are presented with the easy, quick fix that promises to solve all of our problems in an instant, without any effort or determined application. And, being the hopeful creatures that we are, we often succumb to the promise and then immerse ourselves in disappointment and negativity when it doesn't work. And throwing the baby out with the bath water in this instance doesn't help either. You can be forgiven for erroneously thinking that having a mentor and getting all this advice is for the losers – for the ones who can't work it out for themselves. What these types of thinkers tend to forget is, that the successful business owner has not been in search of the get rich quick scheme, s/he has been working solidly and determinedly for many years.

That is the beauty of having an honorable and dedicated mentor – you can see very quickly how they work; what approaches they use to their work; how they treat their staff in relation to their work ethic; and what results they get.

In the recesses of our own hearts and minds we all know that hard work, honest application and dedication are what is needed. We all know that success comes to those who have hung in longer than the rest, or better than the best or in more successful ways than the rest. So finding and following a mentor who mirrors our own beliefs and values, will be the best way you can get to go forward. You will discover the ways and means your mentor has used to overcome setbacks that may still be plaguing you. You will also discover the ways in which other people go about solving problems – it can be an eye opener that could result in amazing success for you.

Business success

It's simple – do you want to be as successful as a multi-billion dollar real-estate mogul for instance or would a smaller, but still successful developer, be more to your liking? If you want to be the next mogul, then study them, their methods, their advice, their work ethic. One of the most famous ones believes, for example, that having a lunch break is a waste of time and never has one unless it's business related. He simply has a sandwich and drink sent up to him. Is this a tip or tactic that you could use to improve your productivity? If it is, and you implement the same principle, then in some small way, the mogul has become a mentor of yours.

Find the business owner, industry leader whose success you wish to emulate and aim for that level, if that is where you want to be. If your goals are less ambitious, then study the leaders anyway – you may find some interesting tidbits that can help you out.

The whole aim of having a mentor is to find out about methods, ways and means of getting ahead without becoming bogged down in the problems that have beset business owners in your industry since the dawn of time. These problems have already been overcome. These problems have already been solved – you don't have to be the savior and solve them all over again. Why would you want to?

Influence

If you wish to eventually be considered an industry leader in your own right, then you are going to want to choose a mentor/s with some influence in your sector. By associating with this mentor and mixing within his/her circle you will be adding to your own credibility and picking up vital tips along the way. The old saying, 'if you lie down with dogs, you get up with fleas' applies in reverse in this scenario. If you associate with the best, you will become the best. It's as simple as that.

Whether you care to admit it or not, each of us has a sphere of influence where what we say, do or proclaim, gets noticed. Some of our spheres of influence may be bigger than others, but influence you have – use it wisely. And of course increase it by associating with the best. What you concentrate on is what you become.

TYPES OF MENTORS

In essence there are as many types of mentors as there are personality types. So you need to decide which type best suits you and your objectives. If you wish to be known as the kind, benevolent, wise worker of miracles who works at a steady and even pace, then find a mentor who is greatly successful by operating this way. If you are a 'highest energy wins' business owner, then you will of course seek out a mentor with the same values, one who is always on the move, always creating, building, shaping, moving.

There is no point in setting someone up as a mentor if you know that there is no way that your style and personality can match with theirs. It becomes a lesson in futility. Sure, it's great to want to operate the way a particular person does, but if in the nuts and bolts of it, they are different from you in every conceivable way, then chances are your progress will be minimal, unless of course you choose to remain loyal to your new standards and methods no matter what.

The barter mentor

Finding this type of mentor is easier than you may think. Just go to the barter network and find the top traders. They are easy to spot. They are usually lauded within the network and they are the ones who are experts in creating their wealth by using trade dollars instead of cash dollars.

Find one. Ask them how they first got started and what they did to grow their business. Ask them about the best ways to use barter, and what to reserve cash for. Ask them as many questions as you can think of about their use of barter so that in the asking and listening to the response, you too, become an expert in its use. There are methods and practices that successful people use, that the ordinary folk among us don't know about. There are ways of making success happen that we may have overlooked or not known about. Find out about all of the ways in which barter can help you. Again – ask, ask, ask.

CHAPTER FIVE

SUMMARY

- A mentor is a guide whom we use to advance our business goals and returns.

- A mentor does not have to be a real person – it can be a theory, an attitude or a style of management.

- We need mentors to fast track us to success and to keep us from veering off course.

- When we find a mentor we want one who is in sync with our own style and personality. A strong mismatch won't work.

- Remember the power of influence – use it, grow it, learn from it.

- Find a barter mentor who is very successful – s/he will be full of tips to use in your business to create on-going success.

CHAPTER SIX

CREATING A WINNING TEAM

> *If the only tool you have is a hammer,*
> *you tend to see every problem as a nail.*
>
> —Abraham Maslow

There has been so much written about teams, winning and getting it together cooperatively with your work colleagues, that this could almost be obsolete before it is even written. However, there are some questions that you may consider before dismissing the need for more information on teams.

Are your employees, people, suppliers, contractors, and other relevant personnel who are integral to your success, allied to your cause? Are they working with you in achieving your goals or are you always having to reign them in to keep them in line with what you want and need? Are your people empowered and energized about your success or are they just there for the paycheck? Are you fed up with just doing it all yourself anyway? If any one of these questions has made you think twice about your team, then perhaps it is worth reading on to find out how to keep them involved and in sync with your objectives.

It is no secret that the most successful businesses have great teams associated with them. They have invested time in their people and their people have returned the favor by working in concert to produce the best results. If your 'team' doesn't feel like a dream or wonder winners, then perhaps the following is more relevant than you realized.

THE WINNING TEAM

There are particular characteristics that are common to many winning teams. There can be a lot of commonalities, but the ones that tend to be more important, are these:

- The personalities of the team.
- The actions of the team.
- The support for others.
- The cohesion of the group.

They may seem self-evident, but it is surprising how often these small details are overlooked or ignored. But, when problems arise it is almost always in one of the above areas that they occur.

The personalities

There are countless personality tests, questionnaires, tips, tricks, warnings and suggestions about the type of person it is best to have on your team. Rather than bogging yourself down with the intricacies and details of these, suffice it to say, that the type of person you really want on your team, is the person who is already there.

You want the worker – the one who loves getting in there and getting it done. This is the person who will get you over the line when there are deadlines to meet, and crunch times to push beyond. They are invaluable and a huge asset. However, they do have their draw backs. They are focused on the job and getting things done, true, but they are bored with goals, plans and the nitty gritty of the 'whole big picture', so having just this type of personality on your team won't be enough. You'll always be dragging them uphill in terms of future visions and problem solving.

You want the complainer – yes believe it or not, the right type of complainer is just what your business needs. By the 'right type' of complainer, we mean, the constructive criticiser. This is the type of worker who always sees problems before they arise. They can see the pitfalls, the setbacks and the complaints that could arise from situations before they come to pass. Oftentimes, they are considered a pain in the neck by their colleagues, but used effectively, this type of personality on your team, could save you a lot of money, time, hard work and future problems. This personality is the one who has to be on planning teams and in development groups – and their input has to be considered. There is a difference though between having a constructive criticiser on board and a real moaner whose life's ambition is to be the pain in everyone's side, just for the sake of it – this type of personality is the extreme of the former complainer, and really should not be on your team, unless they can see that there is a dizzy limit to being negative.

You want the visionary – this is the personality who is always coming to you and saying things like: 'Have you ever thought of doing it this way', or 'I was just thinking, if you added one of these and changed your templates to this, it may give us a better product.' These are the ones who are always looking forward. They love what they do, but they are driven by the future, not the past. They love the thought of 'what could be.' They are invaluable in setting up future trends and keeping you up with what's happening in your own industry. And a quick tip – listen to both the visionary and the complainer when you are planning the way forward. That way, you get both sides of the picture.

You want the analyst – this is the one who usually drives everyone mad with tiny facts and figures. They always know the tiniest details about every job – and they usually know the projections and forecasts too. They know how long equipment should last before it has to be serviced. They usually know what today's temperature and barometric pressure will be too. They love all that sort of stuff – and you should love them for loving it – this passion for detail that they have, can be a saving grace for your business. So the next time you're tempted to roll your eyes at the thought of having to discuss minutiae with this personality, resist, and get them onside instead. You'll be glad you did.

What is a winning team?

You know you want a team that is a winning combination. You know you will always have frustrations regarding staff, and some concerns will be more serious than others. But you also know that those businesses that are a huge success always have winning teams. They have teams that are aligned, cohesive, supported, achievement oriented and success driven.

So, for your business, what is a winning team? If you want a winning business, then it will only be as good as your team allows it to be – no matter how much midnight oil you burn. That horrible old saying, 'you are only as strong as your weakest link' has never been truer. It will all come undone with pressure on your weakest employee. If there is too much pressure – there will be a collapse. For you then, what is the winning team? It is the team that works well under pressure, takes the knocks with the wins, comes back ready for more, loves to be where they are and are always there to support one another.

In the form of an analogy, it is the freight train roaring through your industry, carrying, moving forward, going forward while everyone else sleeps. It is the winner. It is the one that makes others gasp. It is your team. You have built it and you have earned it. Now use it.

How do you make one?

Having a winning team is not just about putting the right people on it and then forgetting it. It's more than that, though the people are the central core of a winning combination. It is about the support you give them. It is about the vision you provide for them. It is about the freedom you give them to become stakeholders in their own future and the future of your business.

Taking responsibility for your own success and that of your team is the first place to start in building a championship team. It's true that the leadership you deliver will come back to you in one form or another. If you're a great leader – you'll have a great team. If you're a leader who is struggling with keeping it all together, then that is what your team will be like. Whether you like it or not – the team you have now is the team you have built according to your strengths and weaknesses. If you are able to look at your team and feel confident in what they are doing for you and the business, then you have done well. If, however, you look at them with dismay and wonder what on earth went wrong, then it's time take stock and look at how to change things for the better.

Just as there are different personality types that make up a good team in all its wonderful diversity, so too are there different types of bosses or leaders who bring their own personality to bear on their team. Some business owners are more one than the other and of course, it is possible to be a combination of the following.

The absentee owner
This is the owner who is so busy running away and hiding from his/her business and responsibilities, that they are never accountable, reliable, contactable or available. This is the guy who is always so busy being somewhere else that the beleaguered managers are literally tearing their hair out to try to manage a failing business. This is the type of leader whose actions are based on fear. S/he knows that the business is failing and they are being reactive rather than pro-active. There is basically no way in the world that this business will be able to prosper, no matter what corrective measures are put in place – short of handing the business over to someone else. This business owner is just waiting for the final curtain basically, and their actions show it.

Some absentee owners can turn things around, but they have to be committed to turning things around rather than running from their fears and problems. And yet it is remarkable how long a sustained bleed can last – some businesses haemorrhage for years before they finally die. The ramifications for your team, for an absentee owner is that this is the best type of leader a team could want – if they don't really want to work that is. And there are some workers who don't really care that much if they don't do a lot of work – as long as they take home the pay check each week, they're not that bothered about performance indicators, goals, schedules, production and output or whatever else may come up. They come in. They do the least amount possible, and with little or no supervision, and then they go home. Great living for some. There are some teams that have up to 60% of their workers who operate in just this way. No wonder the haemorrhage is uncheckable.

The workforce, the team morale, the connection between staff members, will be a direct reflection of what the owner has set up. If the owner thinks so little of the business as to avoid it at all costs, why should the staff feel any differently?

The frightened owner

There are some business owners, usually women, who are so frightened of having to deal directly with staff in a negative way, that they divest themselves of any authority and allow the staff to do, be or have whatever they want. The lunatics are running the asylum, for want of a better analogy and the boss has vacated the premises – emotionally and professionally at least. You can recognise these bosses because of their use of phrases such as, 'Oh we can't have that ready for you because we have several staff on leave,' or ' my admin officer will let me know when I can have those reports and then I'll be able to get back to you, if that's OK.' These are the type of boss who is always asking for permission to exist. They use questions and suggestions rather than directives and never expect accountability from anyone. They are working for their employees and everyone knows it except them. They find themselves exhausted at the end of everyday because they have not only been trying to run the business, but they have run themselves ragged by trying to keep everyone happy. In the end they command no respect, have no loyalty from staff and always end up taking the fall for anything that goes wrong. Their financial situation is rarely good – they have given in to pressure for more wages for less responsibility and so on.

There is a story of one business owner who went to a personal coach to get advice about strengthening her business. During the coaching sessions she began to realize that for years she had been giving the staff exactly what they had wanted, whenever they wanted it, in whatever form they wanted it. She knew the business wasn't doing that well, but it was okay – for now. The 'a-ha' moment came for her when she realized that she was being manipulated by all the staff and that she had been running scared for a long time. During the discussion session with the group at the coaching meeting, she made the grand announcement that when she got back to work on Monday she was going to sack all of them and start again. This shock decision ran through the room in a nano-second and the coach felt he should stay the execution of the workers for the sake of their families and so on. However, he did agree that it would not be possible for the situation to continue as it had done.

He suggested that, let's call her Marie, talk to the staff about the new directions the business would be taking – especially about the new expectations that would be placed on staff. If workers felt they could be a part of this dynamic and streamlined success team, then they would be welcome to stay. If they felt, however, that they would not be able to contribute in the way they would be expected to, along with schedules, accountability and team work, then they would regretfully be allowed to take up other opportunities elsewhere, with Marie's blessing.

What you sow is what you will reap, whether you want to believe it or not. You can make up a thousand excuses to salve your pain, but the bottom line is, what you get from your team is what you have created. If you don't like what you see, it is possible to change it.

The owner dictator

The last two types of business owner/boss have been the frightened type whose hypersensitivity to difficult situations has led them to make some bad decisions. However, they are not the only ones out there who are able to make bad decisions about staff and how to treat them. On the flip side of being scared of your staff is the dictator boss who sees it as his/her life's work to make things difficult for their staff, so they can keep things in check.

For this type of boss, things are never done right unless he/she is hovering over the staff watching every move they make. Staff are never to be trusted because all they really want is to 'rip you off'. This boss rarely gives credit where it is due and he/she is feared by most of his employees. Staff turnover is high and the cost to the business is also high. And surprise, surprise, for this boss, staff act just in the ways he/she expects them to. Staff only do as little as they can get away with and those who would want to impress the boss, have long learned that nothing they can do will ever be good enough, and they have done as the others have done and moved on.

It is this type of boss who can degenerate into the workplace bully and this is also the one who thinks that everyone else is whining sissy who doesn't know a good deal when he's on one. No amount of reasoning will turn this boss around and in the end, the workplace is only a happy place to be when the boss is away – which is hardly ever. All of the staff are well-acquainted with the boss's story and know almost word for word how hard he/she has had to work to get the business to where it is today. This type of boss gets just what he/she deserves from his workers.

The laissez-faire owner

This type of owner could almost be confused with the frightened owner. They are the ones who don't really care if a job is done one way or another, as long as it gets done in the long run. This is the type of owner who isn't really fussed about making hard or tough decisions, as long as everyone is happy and the 'family' is getting on and everything is sunshine and roses.

This type of boss is difficult to work for because there are no hard and set rules as such. This boss makes the fundamental error that people know how to make decisions and get things done with little or no instruction from them. For many workers there is nothing worse than the boss who expects them to work out for themselves how to get things done and in what order. It can be a very confusing workplace and it is no surprise that production and output in a workplace such as this is often low and the quality not as consistent or as high a standard as similar businesses.

In some ways this boss can be described as being so heavenly minded that he/she is of no earthly use. Their vision is always fixated on the beauteous wonders of their make-believe world, that they are immune to the needs of their workers for good solid leadership and direction. At least with the dictator, you know what you have to do, how to do it, when it is to be done by, and by whom. With the laissez-fair boss, it can get a bit wishy washy and again staff turnover is the big loser – as is the business ultimately.

When the business fails for this boss he/she will be off making all sorts of ethereal excuses for the downfall – without ever having had to face him/herself in the mirror. It's the economic downturn. It's the unavailability of credit. It's the housing market. It's the colour of the flowers in the council park.

The pragmatic owner
This is getting on to the best type of boss to have – with some exceptions. This is the boss who beyond everything else is practical, no nonsense, gets things done but without the bullish attitude. In essence this is the boss who is task oriented rather than people oriented – not that they don't like people per se, just that they really enjoy the feeling of ticking

boxes on the to-do list. It gives them a great sense of accomplishment and they don't see why their staff shouldn't feel or do the same.

The one draw-back with this type of boss is that they can often miss the personal side to staffing, not realising that each employee is a human being with their own responsibilities and stories. They can sometimes look confused when the family situations of staff encroach on the workplace.

The firm-but-fair owner

This is the boss with his/her eye on the ball, and on the end result. They are aware of the personal side of their staffing issues and they realize they have to make some considerations for staff and their family situations and the like. However, they never lose sight of the end game. They are always set on achieving the goal, on-time, on budget and on target. This boss will tell his staff, firmly but fairly, to get on with things, lift their game if they need to and sort themselves out.

This is the boss staff will go to because they know he/she will give them a fair hearing and ultimately do what is right. This boss doesn't molly coddle, make excuses or play surrogate parent. They are what they are – a boss in an achieving workplace and work is the place to work – but support and encouragement and reward also play a part in their managerial processes.

As stated above, most bosses would be a combination of two or more styles. The advancing boss is the one who can recognise their faults and be adult enough to face issues head on for the benefit of the whole team and ultimately for the success of the business. No-body likes to see a venture fail, least of all the one who was brave enough to set it up in the first place.

AGREEING ON GOALS

Heading up a winning team is quite a privilege – but it is the same as many things – you get out of it what you put in to it. If you are supportive, generous with your comments and actions and demonstrate to the team that they are valued, needed and capable, then a winning team is well on the way to being formed. However, even with the best of teams, agreeing on goals, time frames, schedules, accountability, team ethos and the like, can be confusing and often times unattainable.

Before you can urge your team to agree on goals, you have first to be convinced that the goals you are aiming to achieve are the goals you want. If you're not convinced, then they won't be either. Let's say that one of your major goals for the next six months is to increase revenue for Product X, a tie-pin for example. Within the six months you will want to inspire your marketing team to come up with a marketing plan that will facilitate the increased sales and get everyone else on board to ensure no setbacks befall the plan.

So, the marketing team has been advised, but there are also other projects that they are undertaking concurrently, and this one, while a priority is still on the drawing board and not so vital this week – they will have a closer look at it next week, or maybe early the week after that. There have been no timelines drawn up so, 'urgent' from the boss, does not really mean 'urgent'. It's the middle of summer and research has shown that tie-pins are worn less in summer than winter and pressing the sale of these items in summer, maybe a losing battle anyway. And of course, some the key staff members needed to make this all happen are on leave, and the marketing team will have to wait til they get back before they can get a complete picture of production output and so on and so on. There are always a hundred reasons why something can't work – getting your team aligned so that things will work is what your primary role as boss and team leader is all about.

Before any goals can be targeted, or even established there has to be some sort of common group agreement that goals and their attainment are necessary, are achievable and are in the best interest of everyone concerned. If team members are not able to become aligned with the goals set up by 'the boss' then many problems are certain to arise at all points of the goal achievement process.

Taking a couple of hours out of the workday routine once every months or so to ensure that all team members are aligned with what is happening in your business, is one of the best things you can ever do for your own success. Thinking that they won't want to know, or that you can't take them away from their duties for this type of thing will ultimately lead to greater costs to you in the long run, such as lost time in fixing problems, lost wages because staff are not being informed of their roles and are taking more days off than they should and it all looks like one big confused mess.

Getting staff on side to realize that if they are all aligned to help achieve the goals, is one of the most important things a boss has to do. It is a huge part of steering the team and the business to greater success. If the team is so uninspired that they couldn't really be bothered achieving your goals, then you have some serious problems that need addressing as soon as possible.

CHOOSING THE TEAM

It's great to be able to look around in your workplace and feel good about the choices you have made. All of your hard work is paying off and your success, if not assured, is at least on the cards in a very positive way. But there are some serious considerations to be made about your team here. If you are carrying dead wood, if you are being held up because of bad performance on the part of employees, if you are always having to 'push the boulder uphill', if you are always in some sort of non-productive conflict with some team members, then cut them loose.

It may be difficult to get rid of some employees, especially if they have been with you for a long time, but in the long run, you will be much better off financially, personally, emotionally and productively. It has been researched long and well that there are at least 18% of your staff who are actively disengaged. This means that almost two out of 10 workers are only there to collect the pay check and do as little as they can do without getting fired. This is the percentage group you should be looking to get rid of. They don't do you any good. They are bad for general morale. They try to convince others to disengage and they are a poor advertisement for your business. If they have been with you for a long time, then the more reason to release them as soon as you can. They have already done untold damage and they will continue to do so as long as you let them.

Having staff who are not aligned to your goals and objectives just holds you back. Certainly you need different personality types to move your business forward, but you need them to be aligned with your future directions. The 18% who are actively disengaged will always be thwarting your progress. They will undermine you and set up imaginary problems at every turn. They don't want progress. They are happy with the way things are. They don't want to move forward and learn new things – this would interfere with their slothfulness and practised indolence. Cut them off now.

WORKING FAST – ALIGN YOUR ENERGIES

Working fast as a team should not be equated to working carelessly or lackadaisically. If it has been agreed that Task A should reasonably take three hours to complete and nine hours later it is still not done, then questions should rightly be raised. If impediments are continually hindering the achievement of your goals and your team is not in any hurry to eradicate them, then 'the boss' needs to sort this out. The phrase 'most energy most done' is not lost here. If your team is highly motivated, aligned, achievement oriented and supportive of the business and each other, then high energy and great results must follow. It is a given. But if there is constant confusion, passing of the proverbial buck, unwillingness to see things through to their conclusion, uncertainty about individual roles etcetera, then the vital productive cohesive energy that the team needs to win, is dissipated and lost in the quagmire of who does what, when and where.

If your team is not accustomed to achieving goals fast, then teach them. Take small projects first and celebrate the wins that come from that. Gradually extend the terms and circumstances so that small achievable goals soon become large achievable goals and all team members are winners and ultimately the business is able to move from success to greater success.

GOAL ACHIEVING

The meetings at the local Chamber of Commerce used to run like this. Committee members would gather at 6.30 pm on the second Wednesday of every month, some with bottles of wine, others with crackers and dips and some with more substantial repasts. The meetings would go on for hours and usually many of the items on the agenda had to be carried over to the next meeting because the committee did not have the time to consider them.

Much to-do and furore and fuss was caused with the election of a new president to the committee who banned the consumption of alcohol at meetings, insisted on the strict adherence to agenda items only, raised the standard of minute taking and finished meetings by 8.30 pm each session. The fallout was instant. There were those who were incensed by the arrogance of the new president in dismissing practices that had been in place for years. Some were so adamant they were not going to support the new regime that they resigned on the spot. Others found all sorts of things to be upset about and proceeded to inform members that things had gone terribly awry. But a strange thing happened as a result. The void that was left by complaining resigning committee members was filled by those who also wanted to get things done in an organized and competent manner. Agenda items were actually being dealt with. The press began to take renewed interest in the Chamber and events that had been planned for years were actually happening. The renewed energy in the group was remarkable and what had begun as a negative reaction to new circumstances, soon changed to appreciation for a job well done.

When you get a group of people together in a room to talk, then that is just what they tend to do, and the social aspect within us all can take over and important things that were meant to be discussed can get overlooked. How many times have you walked out of a meeting thinking 'well that was a waste of time.' And yet time is the one thing that we should never give away lightly – you can never get it back, you can never recycle it and you can never have enough of it. To squander it because of some social chatter or inane ramblings is wasteful to the extreme, non-productive, an example of poor leadership and totally undesirable. And yet, for so many frivolous reasons we give our time away unthinkingly. It has been researched and shown that most bosses only spend 10% of each day on income producing activity. The rest of the working day is taken up with chatting, solving personal problems, attending to minor problems, answering communications and sitting in meetings.

If only 10% of what you do is centred on producing income, then it is no wonder that over 80% of businesses fail in the first five years.

When you schedule a meeting, it should be made known to attendees before they even enter the room that some things are not-negotiable.

- Tardiness will not be accepted.
- Once the meeting has begun, all attendees agree to be mentally 'present'.
- Team members agree to endorse the company's code of conduct.
- Agenda items will be submitted at least a day beforehand.
- All those involved in the meeting will agree to have the business and agenda items as the sole focus of the meeting.

- Members will be encouraged to call each other to account if discussions waver from the point.
- No social chatter shall be part of the meeting process, except before and after the meeting as agreed.
- All agenda items will be dealt with according to timelines, persons responsible and objectives outlined.

Your business and its success must come first. If it doesn't, if it is constantly being pushed to the back seat because of some social chit chat or problem, then ultimately your failed business will be responsible for losing all of your jobs and then there really will be something worth talking about.

Just as a side note here it is interesting to mention that those businesses who provide great 'buffets' at meetings with champagne and hors d'oeuvres and the like are often the ones who fail the soonest. It's one thing to make your staff feel appreciated, it's another to confuse the art of doing business with a social occasion. If you want to socialise with staff and give them a good time, then do it outside of meeting times. Keep the boundaries clear for everyone. It will be a lot more productive for your business when you do.

THE WINNING TEAM AND BARTER

All of the above-mentioned factors are essential to the winning team. No team can be efficiently and professionally achieving great results if they are not aligned and cohesive. But there is one other factor that is common to many high-energy winning teams and that is the use of barter.

Without the addition of barter in the whole business equation, the pressure to perform can be extreme and overwhelming. The pressure on the incoming and outgoing dollar can also be intense. It is the result of being under so much constant financial pressure that can lead business owners and bosses into making reactive and ill-planned actions that have detrimental effects on everyone.

With the use of barter however, there is an easing of pressure. There isn't so much direct pressure on the incoming dollar – it doesn't have to do as many things as it would do without barter. For instance without barter the incoming dollar would have to be paying all the outgoings, including salaries, utilities, rent, advertising, incentives, equipment, stock and so on. With barter there are a whole lot of items that can be paid for with barter, including equipment, incentives and advertising.

Beating yourself and your business up without the use of barter just doesn't make any sense. If there was a way to increase your cash flow, divert cash dollars to better uses, relief in the form of alternative payment methods and access to a worldwide barter community, why on earth wouldn't you want to be a part of that.

CHAPTER SIX

SUMMARY

- Creating a winning team is up to the leader.

- Making excuses simply masks the objectives and keeps you from succeeding.

- There is room on your team for diverse personality types – use them to your advantage.

- What type of business owner are you and how do your strengths and weaknesses affect the productivity of your team.

- Having clear and achievable goals is the best way to get ahead.

- Working according to timelines and schedules is a good way to keep on track and keep team members accountable.

- Most energy, most done – keep your team motivated and moving.

- Time-wasters in meetings cost you big time.

- Working without the support of barter in your team, makes for increased pressure and more stressed workers.

CHAPTER SEVEN

MAKING THE MOST OF YOUR MARKETING BUDGET, PART I

You can fool all the people all the time if the
advertising is right and the budget is big enough.
—Joseph E. Levine

Every single business owner on the planet knows that even if their product is the best one available, it will only sell if other people, the beloved customers, know about it. And of course, the only way to let your customers know about your whizz-bang product is to advertise it. And that's where the big bucks come in. Even a not so major company like Harvey Norman International spends over US$250m per year on advertising. That's a big bucket of funds the company has to dip into, and totally beyond the level of imagination of most small- to medium-sized businesses.

But, here's the thing – it's not the size of the budget that's important. It's not the huge amount they spend annually that is supposed to dazzle us. It's the fact that they have a budget, one that is renewed each year that is dedicated solely to advertising and or marketing. Well, that's obvious, one could argue. And it becomes almost laughable to imagine a big business without a marketing budget. It's like walking around on one leg when you don't have to.

So, why then is it laughable when you ask the owner of a small- to medium-sized business how big their advertising and marketing business is? The response is the same time and time again. 'Marketing budget? I can't even pay my bills, let alone put things aside for marketing – who am I, Rockefeller?' And with snide and defensive comments like that, they hide behind every excuse under the sun to avoid having to get into the advertising argument.

They know they have to advertise. They know they should be dedicating a proportion of their income to the advertising and marketing budget. They know the benefits that could result from a comprehensive well managed marketing plan. They know that the successful companies all have a marketing budget and use it wisely. What they don't know is how to make the most of their marketing dollar. They don't know what's a fair price to pay and they don't know when enough is enough. They are sick to the back teeth of being harassed by a dozen different sales people a day hawking their deal of the century, either by phone, or by pushing, unannounced, into their office. At first they realize they have to be known 'out there' and agree to pretty much every offer that comes along – always being promised that the revenue they will receive from the ad will pay for the ad. But it rarely works that way, and at the end of the month they are faced with bills for thousands of dollars that resulted in very few, if any sales.

So when next month rocks along and they are approached by the next set of advertising hopefuls, they angrily say no and dismiss the offers out of turn. Then of course, they are given the hard sell again and when they refuse again, they are given the look – the one that yells out across the town, 'Loser! Loser! Loser!' And what hurts the most is not the deprecating look or attitude, it's the fact that deep down inside, that's exactly how the business owner feels. S/he knows that business should be booming because they have been intelligent enough to engineer their own success. But when the reality of the situation hits them between the eyes and they realize they don't have the money to spend on luxuries like advertising, then it can become a continuum of devastation and desperation.

One of the biggest mistakes that business owners make is thinking that advertising and marketing budgets are for the big guys. Another big mistake is thinking that the whole world of advertising is so complex and daunting that it would be an even bigger mistake to get involved in trying to understand it.

But how would you feel if you were to buy, say a café where you were happy to sell the best coffee in the region, and then you refused to learn how to make the best coffee you could. Instead of learning how to use the wonderful espresso machine that had already built up a good reputation, you simply brewed the coffee beans in a pot on the stove and then expected your customers to love it, sans crema, sans correct temperatures and sans the specialized treatment it deserves. You would be laughed out of business. You know, you have to learn how it all works – your business depends on it. You don't become a quarry owner and then learn how to crochet, convinced that a good crochet technique will win you more customers.

The same applies to advertising and marketing within your business. You don't simply do whatever you feel like at the time, call it marketing, pray for good results and expect your business to succeed, when the efforts you have put in have had nothing to do with real marketing. You would be laughed out of business.

There are some business owners who like to think that their business is above and beyond the rules – that their business doesn't have to play by the rules of the ordinary folk. Their business is going to somehow be catapulted to fame and fortune because of who they are. Unfortunately many of them learn too late, that the rules of advertising and marketing apply just as much to them as to anyone.

THE DIFFERENCE BETWEEN ADVERTISING AND MARKETING

Many times the terms are used interchangeably and for the most part, in the general scheme of things that's fine. Everybody knows pretty much what you mean and the world goes on. However, for our intents and purposes here, and for your extended knowledge and intelligent use of your marketing and advertising budget, it is important to know the difference between the two terms and what each one will cost you.

Advertising

This is the nuts and bolts of the game. Advertising is:

- The print ad.
- The advertorial.
- The television commercial.
- The two-page feature in the local paper.
- The radio ad.
- The flyers.
- The direct-mail drop.
- Brochures.

But the lines can get a little blurry when you think that every promotion you run, every open day, every comment and endorsement, are all part of advertising your product or service. But strictly speaking when you are talking about an advertising budget, the features listed above, are what you are actually talking about. And in essence your advertising budget will be a part of your marketing budget.

Marketing

Marketing is the general picture, the overall umbrella under which you will promote your business. These days this one little world has come to incorporate a lot of other terms, the sum of which could and does take up masses of space on shelves under definitions, glossaries, sections, aspects, acronyms and so on. This is one of the major reasons the average business owner can and is overwhelmed by the subject. The jargon within the marketing industry alone is akin to speaking a whole other language.

All you really need to know about marketing per se is that it is *the whole business approach to selling your product or service* and that every successful business should have a comprehensive and workable marketing plan that is in use daily, and not simply decorating the bookshelf or propping up a desk.

SAMPLE MARKETING PLAN

Putting together an effective marketing plan could set you back tens of thousands of dollars if you have professional marketers do it for you – and if you have that sort of money to invest, then by all means do so, but please ensure that the marketing team stays involved long enough to instruct the business owners and management about what is involved in the whole process.

If, however, you don't have the excess cash to spend on having one done for you, then don't despair, there are basic areas that you and your managers can cover yourselves. The thing to remember is that there are certain aspects that should be covered by your marketing plan if you want a comprehensive marketing of your product or service.

Some of the most important things you should include in your marketing plan are:

Your marketing vision – how do you envision your business and what is your ultimate goal for it. The vision for Starbucks for instance is: First and foremost, ... to 'establish ourselves as the premier purveyor of the finest coffee in the world while maintaining our uncompromising principles while [we] grow(s).'

1 Goals.
2 Purpose.
3 Overview.

The ideal customer – Describe your ideal customer and know all about him/her: (Some high-profile businesses name their ideal customer – Andrew, or whatever, so they really feel they have an emotional investment in doing business with them.)

1 Who are they.
2 Where do they live.
3 Who do they associate with.

4   What are their hobbies.

5   What is their level of income.

6   How much do they spend on goods and services like yours.

7   What problems are they having.

8   How can you be their salvation.

Differentiating ourselves from competitors

1   How is your business different.

2   What makes you stand out from your competitors.

3   What knowledge do you have that will give you an advantage.

4   How can you serve/help your customers better than your competitors.

Strategies

1   Expand distribution outlets – open more stores.

2   Launch innovative new products.

3   Overseas market – is it viable.

4   Develop a joint venture.

5   Explore niche markets.

Product innovation

1   Would the simple tweaking of your product and its presentation be sufficient to generate more sales or invite a price increase?

2   What can you value-add immediately to your product (little or no real cost to you, but a high perceived value to your customer)?

Marketing sources

1   Hard-copy magazines.

2   Television.

3   Radio.

4   Mail drops.

5   Direct mail.

6   School bulletin.

7   Sponsor a team or event.

8   Corporate sponsorships.

Web strategies

1   Blogs.

2   Articles.

3   E-zines.

4   Social media.

5   Press releases.

6   YouTube.

Getting quality leads

1   Buy lists.

2   Build your own lists.

3   Affiliate with other businesses and use their lists.

Converting quality leads

1   *VALUE ADD* – Add value to your product or service – the popularity of adding a set of free steak knives didn't happen because people were eating more steak – it happened because people love to feel rewarded for their purchase. They love to feel they have something extra for nothing. However, if the value-add is in keeping with your product and costs you little or nothing then so much the better.

2   *FREQUENCY OF CONTACT* – The power of your influence decreases by 10% for every month that you do not contact your clients – so if you only contact them every six months, you have lost 60% of your influence with them each time you connect.

Risk reversal

1   *GUARANTEES* – Never be afraid of adding a guarantee to your product or service. It instills confidence and adds credlbility.

2   Don't make it hard for your customer to pay you. There is nothing more frustrating than trying to purchase something and you have to jump through a dozen hoops to do it – and then there are no guarantees you will ever see the product or have the chance of getting your money back. The number of small businesses who refuse to use merchant facilities in their businesses because it incurs a 2% charge from their bank is astounding – what they don't realize is that they are missing out on big purchases by not having it. And losing 2% of $1,000 is better than losing all of $1,000.

Continuity – This is a much under-used, yet extremely lucrative marketing and income producing strategy. What it means is that you have attached a program of continual payment to the sale of your product. It is ingenious and yet so under utilized. Basically, this is how it works – you buy a set of premium tires (or whatever product or service you want to include here) and for $25 per month (just an example) which is an automated direct debit, you will be entitled to regular tire checks, one free tire per 12 months and inclusion into the VIP Gold Member Auto Club. You are free to opt out at any time.

Marketing calendar – Simply stated, this is a month by month outline of what you will be doing to market your business. For instance: March: Get ready for the holiday campaign – print flyers, advertise in the local paper, redo the menus, adjust pricing and so on. Every business should have its marketing calendar on the office wall for all employees to see, There should never be any surprises about what's coming up next week or next month.

Forecasts – This is where the number crunchers come in and you all decide that if you get so many new customers per month, at XYZ cost then you should be able to enjoy ABC% growth and TRS% profit. One of the biggest pitfalls in this area is that there is often a difference between the real profits and the forecasted profits – and this is also when a lot of business owners and managers and accountants throw their arms up in horror declaring 'It didn't work. It didn't work' and start bemoaning doom and gloom. Sometimes the difference between a small profit and a huge one can be something as simple as one word in the ad's headline. Instead of giving up straight away and losing a potential fortune, keep tweaking and testing and if it still doesn't work, then ask your customers what's wrong – they'll soon tell you. Then LISTEN TO WHAT THEY SAY AND FIX IT.

Accountability and audits – It's easy to make up pretty plans and strategies and watch them unfold and then sit back and point the finger at someone else when the forecasts and projections fall well short of the results. That's why grown ups apply and abide by accountability strategies that keep people responsible. When your name is on a project and your signature is on the check and your reputation is on the line, you will more than likely work twice as hard to ensure your results are good – and you if you really don't care, then you should be looking for work elsewhere. It's that simple.

It's one of the reasons too, that companies and businesses are required to have independent audits on a regular basis. It keeps everyone accountable and supposedly keeps them honest.

YOUR MARKETING BUDGET

So, now we have defined and discussed the difference between advertising and marketing and set out your basic marketing plan. Now it's time to talk about your marketing budget.

Far from having tens of millions of dollars budgeted every year for marketing, most small to medium businesses have a small amount set aside each month, and there are some of course, that have no budget for marketing whatsoever. They simply spend money on marketing and ads where ever and when ever they see fit. One regional shoe shop owner, keen to be seen supporting the community is in debt to the tune of $15,000 a month. His monthly sales don't even cover half of that. It's easy to see how a failing business can get very ugly very soon.

The best way to approach the subject of a marketing budget is to make a definite sum available at regular times. Some examples of basic marketing budgets are as follows:

1 10% of weekly incomings
2 $3,000 per month every month
3 $40,000 budget available at the beginning of each year – and when it's gone it's gone
4 All revenue raised from product RZ will be the marketing budget

The only problem with the budget examples above is that they all rely on the availability of cash. And this is where big troubles start from little acorns. There is no allocation for advertising, a sales rep from the local paper comes in and extols the virtues of the latest great deal for advertisers, a two-for-one offer which includes advertorial and so on. You know it's a good deal and you take it. Next thing you know, the account is in. There has been no influx of customers as promised. The ad has long since been forgotten and you have yet another bill that is impossible to pay.

Your marketing budget and barter

What if your marketing budget could be sizeable, regular and not reliant on cash? Wouldn't that free up your thinking about marketing and take the pressure off? Wouldn't it be great to have the spare cash flow to use on business necessities such as wages and utilities? Wouldn't it be nice to be able to plan for profits rather than sitting back in the dark corner and praying for a visit from the good fairy?

So, when it comes to advertising and marketing you can pretty much get by without using any cash dollars at all. And during times of economic hardship, when other businesses are really hurting and cutting back on their advertising, thus jeopardizing their market presence, savvy business owners are using barter to up their advertising spend, increase their market awareness and presence, and cash in on the opportunities that others don't have the money to get involved in.

You know how there is sometimes talk about the 'lucky ones' who always seem to do well, regardless of the 'times'? Well, it's not about luck or being in the right place at the right time. It's about making your own luck, being in any place you choose at whatever time suits you, because you are almost immune to misfortune because of your good planning.

Just about every kind of advertising method has a barter trader. So you can have the television ads running. It is possible to engage in a radio campaign. You can have flyers, brochures, new menus, newsletters, manuals, reports and projections printed for no cash outlay. You can improve your results time and time again without having the nightmare of deciding between advertising costs and paying staff!

However – and isn't there always at least one! Your barter budget is not limitless either and you will still need to make the most of your advertising budget. It's not like pouring water down the drain and expecting nothing in return except an empty pitcher. When you're advertising, you do expect a return. You do expect to see something back in exchange for your beautiful water. You do want profit and you do want success. If you don't then you are enjoying running a hobby and not a business.

So let's take an advertising budget of say, $5,000 barter and see just what we can do with it. We'll start with online marketing – that's marketing and not just advertising.

ONLINE MARKETING AND ADVERTISING

Of your $5,000 barter you want to allocate $500 to online marketing. You have a website and you are already receiving emails and the like. But that's as basic as your system is and you realize that you could do a lot more on line. You're not sure how to go about it so you do the following:

1 You set up a *blog* **page** (a blog is like setting up a worldwide diary or journal online. You write about the things that interest you, in this case your business – door handles for example and you talk about the types of door handles, the production processes that are preferred by quality suppliers, the costs that can vary and why, the color results from different manufacturing processes and so on and so on. So when someone keys in 'door handles' for their search, your blog may come up in their search, depending on the key words you and they have used. The customer checks out your blog, clicks on the backlinks to your site and you have the possibility of welcoming a new customer to your lists.).

Advantages of a blog: it sets you us as an 'expert' in your field. It gives you credibility, especially if there are comments left by intelligent users. It puts your 'word' out there in the common marketplace and is basically another easy way of attracting customers back to your site.

COST: FREE.

2 You write up some *articles for publication online*. This is not as daunting as it may sound. The general length of an article is between 300–500 words. That's about a page of typing, size 12 font, 1.5 line spacing. You put a catchy headline on the top – e.g. 'Seven Ways of Testing for Quality Door Handles'. You include a couple of quotes, not from Shakespeare, but some words of wisdom you may have to add to give the article some credibility. For instance: 'Anton Jefferies, of www.doorhandlesareus.com had this to say of the cheap, unreliable imports that were flooding the market. 'People work hard for their money. To waste it on imports that will only last six months at the longest is a great shame.' Of course, you are Anton Jefferies. You have created your own quote and you have

written the article in the first person, active voice – that means you have written about things from the them and he perspective (I doesn't exist) and all your statements have been action oriented.

Once you have written your article you can do several things with it. You can post it as a blog on your own blog site. You can submit it to several online news distributors or article directories. You can use as a review source in your own website. You can use the article as content in your newsletters and emails and you can archive it towards producing the first volume of your book – *The Tips and Tricks to Choosing the Perfect Door Handles for Your House, and the 10 Dangers to Avoid.* By the way, a well written article can also double as a press release for online papers and directories.

Each and every one of the above uses has backlinks to your site. Each use is designed to raise your profile, bring credibility to your image and enhance customer confidence. But beware one thing – one's it's out there, it's out there for good. So be careful in what you say. Don't make any outrageous promises or threats and certainly keep everything above board and professional. If you discipline yourself to doing one article every ten days – allowing about an hour for the writing and posting of it, you will soon have many avenues out there all leading to your P&L statement.

There are some article distributors that will charge a fee – however, there are still plenty who don't. It's up to you.
COST: FREE.

3 *DVDs, online TV, social networking*: These are all very powerful ways of communicating regularly with your customers. They are informative, exclusive and opt in. They have the great perceived value and opportunities for using them are endless.

Using these media types as part of a loyalty or customer 'club' is very powerful. People want to belong – that's why Facebook,

Twitter, LinkedIn and a host of other social sites are so popular. People love to be a part of the in-group. Most of these media items are either free or very low cost to produce and put online. Always be aware of copyright restrictions however and do not reproduce the work of someone else unless you have the resell rights or have sought permission.

These media items are also a good way to Joint Venture with another business. The two businesses can split the costs and combine data bases. Both of you can add content and gain credibility from and for each other. Be selective with whom you choose to JV, for while their great attributes will also be aligned with you, so too will their failings. And a destroyed relationship can be very hard to build up again.

You may also wish to consider the possibility of forming an arrangement with a supplier in a sponsorship deal. They have their logo and your endorsement, and they pay for the supply of the media event/item.

COST: FREE with sponsorship or up to $100 or so.

4 *Social media*: sounds like a happy fun thing doesn't it and for the most part it can be. The term itself refers to those forms of online media that deal in social interaction between users. The most popular of these are Facebook, Twitter and LinkedIn. And while the primary intent of these sites is to 'chat' and exchange cool information about people and products, savvy business people have also used the sites to promote their own businesses. Short of providing a 5,000-word essay on the best ways of using these sites for your business, let it suffice to say that getting to know how the sites work will result from two things. Your observations of the site and putting up your own pages, and most importantly of all, following the Facebook, Twitter or LinkedIn page of a business or person you admire.

If you remember one thing when you are on these pages, it will go a long way to improving your results and ensuring you maximize your presence. Whenever you sit down to 'chat' on one these sites, you are not you personally. That is to say, whenever you login you should do so with the goal in mind of being the persona of your business. You don't make a comment that could be deemed to be offensive in any way and you don't make yourself look lazy, incompetent, forgetful, inefficient or unattractive in any way. Think of yourself as the epitome of the air steward. Always polite, cheerful, courteous and business-like.

Also, do not provide any information that you would like to have in the hands of an 'enemy' for want of a better word. Keep public domain information in the public domain and private information, private. While these sites may function as a diary or journal for some people, it is not so for any business owner. There are plenty of high profile businesses who have their own pages. Find one or two you would like to emulate and do what they do.

COST: FREE.

5 *YouTube/podcasts/DVDs*: These days, if you haven't noticed that there are cameras everywhere, then you must be living in the last cave known to mankind. There are cheap video cameras, camcorders, digital cameras, phone cameras, and even most of the newer cameras themselves have a video function. It's not necessary to hire the cast of thousands to be featured in a video. Just ask any car dealer.

There are videos available on just about every subject under the sun, made by just about everyone else but you. So, if you want to be the expert in your field, make a video and post it on YouTube, and at the end of every email you send, at the bottom of your invoices or at the bottom of every letterhead, or in a great big sign in your showroom, or playing loop style in the café, let the whole world know you have arrived.

One of the finest chefs in the district has posted a YouTube video on how to fillet a kingfish and how to make meals using truffles. It adds great credibility to his reputation, provides important information for his customers and raises his profile world wide. You can do the same. Just get hold of your teenager or their friends, create the video and upload – it's free. So is producing a podcast and a DVD – except for the same costs that are associated with CDs.

COST: FREE.

So you see, from the $500 of your $5,000 budget for advertising you still have about $300 left – and what's more you have made a huge impact on the world stage. The name of your business is now international as is your influence and your customer base. True it will have cost you some time. But what if you simply exchanged three hours of television time to produce this much awareness. That's a pretty good return in anyone's book.

We have yet to talk about offline advertising. This topic is so extensive that it will be covered more fully in the following chapter. The subject of advertising is so important and so under-rated that in order to do it justice a few lines will not suffice.

CHAPTER SEVEN

SUMMARY

- The subject of advertising and marketing need not be scary, expensive minefield it is often touted to be.

- Advertising is the advert itself.

- Marketing includes the advertisements but also includes a whole business approach to promoting product or service and can encompass the building of brand and image.

- It's always best to work from a marketing plan that is updated regularly.

- A marketing budget does not necessarily need cash to operate effectively.

- It is possible to make a huge impact globally online without the use of any money at all – and if you choose to hire someone to set things up for you, you can use barter dollars and not cash to do so.

- It is possible to make your marketing budget work for you and not against you.

CHAPTER EIGHT

MAKING THE MOST OF YOUR MARKETING BUDGET, PART II

The successful man will profit from his mistakes
and try again in a different way.

—Dale Carnegie

As discussed in the previous chapter, one of the most loosely guarded budgets for most business owners is that of the Marketing Budget, if a business actually has one. For the most part, it generally operates on an ad hoc basis and according to whatever is the 'flavor of the month.' However, successful businesses don't operate this way. They are much more vigilant and organized about their marketing spend and the more successful ones again, will often find a way of Joint Venturing, securing sponsorships or using barter as an intelligent means of offsetting their cash dollar expenditure.

We also discussed the various online methods of advertising and marketing which can be very cost effective indeed. In fact, most of them are free if you choose to create and submit articles, blogs, posts, videos and podcasts yourself. Even if you hire a third party to organize these marketing techniques, it is possible to find businesses who will provide these services using barter, thus preserving cash resources for other needs.

In this chapter we will be discussing the various means available for your offline dollar. And the reason we have selected a complete chapter for this is that the potential for raising your business profile and increasing revenue via advertising is so important that it could mean the difference between make and break in your business. And while it's easy to dismiss a lot of advertising as a useless waste of money, there are indeed ways to ensure your precious investment is used in the correct way with the correct assessment and evaluations and utilizing successful tactics. Ergo, once these options have been clearly outlined for you it will be easier for you to ascertain which method/s of promotion is/are more suitable to your particular needs and business.

HARD-COPY ADVERTISING

When we talk about hard-copy advertising, we mean anything that one is able to physically pick up and read, typically magazines, newspapers, newsletters, brochures, general flyers, postcards, door hangers, invitations, direct-mail pieces and the like. It will usually involve the services of a writer, graphic designer, printer, distributor and/or a postal drop. So, from the start, you can see why a lot of small to medium sized businesses are put off altogether. You could be looking at a minimum spend of $2,000 to $5,000 depending on the number of items you need to produce, or the size of the ad you want to place.

Apart from needing a good bit of extraneous cash reserve to cover these costs, you will also need to be quite organized. For instance if you want to promote your upcoming Valentine's Day dinner at your fab restaurant, then you won't be waiting until the week before to get your flyers out. You will have planned the whole campaign weeks in advance, coordinating your times with the writer, the designer, the printer and the post office. And some need at least two month's notice. Being Disorganized is what a lot of advertisers hope for. They know that if they take the burden from you and do the writing, the designing, the printing, publishing and distribution for you, you will be more than likely to jump on the next best opportunity that comes along. And sometimes that's not a bad thing – it's better than having no advertising out there at all.

However, this is where so many businesses become disillusioned and annoyed with hard copy advertising – with no means of measuring the success of any ad, with no way of deciding who your target market was in a magazine or newspaper, with no real way of knowing what part of the ad worked or didn't work, it's almost impossible to know if your ad worked or didn't work. Some would say that the success of an ad could be measured by the response – that is, the number of extra sales it generated. But unless there is a measurement tool attached to each ad, it really is not possible to know. That's why a lot of businesses will say things like, 'How did you hear about us?' or 'Did you see our ad in the paper this week?' Most of them don't realize that it is possible to measure your ROI on each ad that you produce. And if you have hired a marketing or advertising agency to produce your campaigns for you and they don't offer objective testing results for each ad, then they are not doing their job, and definitely not serving you in the best way possible. Always ask for an evaluation of each ad. It's amazing that some of them will look at you as if you've just asked for the family jewels. Others will gasp and say that it isn't possible. The plain truth is that it is possible. Just how to do this will be explained in more detail in the section below. But for now we'll talk about the types of hard copy advertising that are available and how to make the most of your advertising spend.

MAGAZINES AND TRADE JOURNALS

It would be very rare indeed to get change from $600 for a print ad in any magazine or trade journal. Just ask anyone who has to advertise regularly this way – give your local realtor a call and ask how much they have to spend each week in real estate guide magazines (usually an insert in the local paper). True, they get some discounts and preferred spacing because of the frequency with which they advertise, but they are still up for significant amounts each week. Some offset this by asking the customer to pay for it. In some states that is the norm, but in most states, they have to offset these costs themselves. And if a house is withdrawn they can sometimes be in the red by thousands of dollars.

More often than not, a regular advertiser can fall into one of two categories: firstly they can be truly savvy people, totally aware of what works and what doesn't work. They will know about headlines, copy, colour vs black and white and they will have testing factors in place to record ROI, or secondly they can be just plain lazy and take out whatever ad the sales person suggests would be right at the time. However, you will notice that after some little while, these advertisers either begin to advertise less regularly or they drop off altogether except for special occasion advertising. If you're serious about your business and getting the best results for it, then category one is definitely the place you want to be.

If you are considering purchasing a print ad then these are some of the factors you have to take into consideration.

- How arresting is my headline?
- Will my ad stand out from the others – e.g. will my ad be just one of ten others in the restaurant guide offering the same as everyone else?
- Will my ideal customer notice my ad and be drawn to it?
- What can I add to this advert so I can measure the results – i.e. if I add the offer of Free coffee with every Big Breakfast, bring in this ad to claim your offer, then I know how many people have responded to that ad in particular, and I can measure my response.
- Is there some sort of continuity aspect I can add if the advert is successful?

These questions apply to every advertisement you put out – including the Yellow Pages. If your business is going to be just another example of all the other businesses already in there, then why bother putting an ad at all, except to fill ad space for the advertiser? In general, the sales people you will deal with will have a fairly good knowledge of how to put your ad together and so on, but remember, they are only ever working on their own agenda, and that is to get as much ad space sold for the magazine, newspaper, directory. So, naturally they will be recommending bigger, bolder, more regular presence in their publication, which is not necessarily a bad thing – when it's not your money that's being used. And by the way, did you know that after extensive research on the Yellow Pages, it has been discovered that colored ads don't pull more of a response than the regular black and white ones, so that may be something worth considering the next time you're placing an ad.

Another thing that you may like to note is to remember to take a good long look at the advertisers who take out ads week after week. Unless they're completely flush with funds or quite stupid, they're not going to be wasting their money on repeat advertising that doesn't work. Generally they will have done their homework and figured out already which headline works best, the size of ad that will bring the most return and the copy that draws results. Have a look at what they are saying and more importantly have a very close look at *how* they are saying it. Note too, what they are NOT saying.

As a general idea a full page ad in a leading national magazine can cost you in excess of $40,000. For this kind of money, you would want to make sure that every aspect of your ad was thoroughly covered. For most businesses of course, this is just a ludicrous amount and one that would never be considered. But just because your budget is smaller doesn't mean you have to be any the less serious about ensuring you get the biggest impact for your dollar.

NEWSPAPERS

Advertising in a newspaper, be it local or national, is quite a different ball game from advertising in a magazine, journal or directory. Here, it's much more fast paced and your ad is only extant for as long as the paper is current. That means, depending on frequency of publication, your ad could be the flavor of the week and bringing in hordes til Friday, but after that you're the lining for the budgie cage. That's one of the biggest reasons businesses get frustrated and angry with having to advertise repeatedly. It can seem to be an unceasing, never ending bottomless pit into which thousands upon thousands of dollars are thrown again and again. That's okay if you are getting a great response for the ads, but it's another thing altogether when the response is only mediocre at best.

Some of the frustration that businesses feel can be exemplified in this analogy. If you were to pay a car mechanic to fix and maintain your car for a set amount of dollars each week and after each maintenance session the mechanic was not able to guarantee a successful result for you, would you continue to use the same service? Chances are you would run a mile – you'd have to because the car wouldn't be working!

Why should it be so much different when employing the services of an advertiser – true the analogy falls down a little when we consider market trends and seasonality and economic situations and so on, but in general you get the point.

These days there are another couple of points you may wish to consider before undertaking your newspaper ad campaign. Because of the immediacy of sources like the internet, radio and television, a lot of people would rather read or receive their news information on line or via the flipping of a switch. To surrender your valuable advertising dollars to a source that is not considered all that relevant in some spheres, may be worth a second thought.

Newspapers will not provide you with a results based ad placement – it is up to you as the advertiser to ensure proper measures are set up so you can measure your own ROI.

As a suggestion for a small to medium sized business only run newspaper ads when you are assured of a good deal from the paper – and sometimes they do have some very appealing specials. Always ask for the possibility of an editorial to run with the ad. They will do the obligatory rolling of the eyes and shake their heads and laugh and so on, but sometimes out of the blue they will need a small space of copy to be filled and lo and behold you will be the first to come to mind. And certainly if you are engaging in a lengthy contract with them – make sure that an editorial every couple of months or so is part of the deal.

Ensure that your ad is not just another same-old, same-old. Have headings, offers, guarantees, gimmicks that make your ad stand out from the others. And of course, include some trackable offer that relates to that ad only.

BROCHURES AND GENERAL FLYERS

There are a couple of general 'rules' of advertising that you may wish to note. You have four seconds before someone clicks to another page if your website does not grab their attention and you have approximately eight seconds to harness their attention in a print ad that comes in with the other 'junk' mail. It is six times easier to sell to an existing customer than it is to sell to a new one. Your level of influence with a customer decreases by 10% for each month you are not in contact with them and a slick and glossy brochure or flyer does not necessarily bring in better results than a basic DIY black and white one on colored paper. The ROI for your mail out is usually: 1–2% return okay; 2–5% very good; anything over 5–10% exceptional, so if you're sending out 100 flyers, don't expect to be flooded with orders.

It's one thing for the huge multi-nationals to print weekly catalogues that go to every household in the country, and it's another altogether for a small to medium business to hope to do the same. You know the idea is absurd before you even begin, and here's why. People know that every Tuesday, Wednesday or whatever day of the week it is, they will get the next bundle of 'junk mail'. It is as regular as clockwork and people also know that when big commercial days such as Christmas, Mother's Day, Father's Day and so on, come up, there will inevitably be more of a bundle than usual. Sometimes people will go through the lot and see what there is that is pertinent and appealing to them, or they may simply choose the one or two catalogues that are of general interest to them and discard the rest. Or, if you are like most people, you simply put the whole lot into the bin before even looking at them. And so how on earth is your little flyer supposed to compete with that huge lot? The simple answer is − it can't, it won't and most likely, all that money you've spent on design, printing, distribution and the rest, will just be thrown out. That's the sad and honest truth. You stand a better chance if you organize your leaflet/flyer drop through the post office. Here, at least it has the perception, rightly or wrongly, that your flyer has a little more legitimacy about it than the other flyers. However, you have only a few seconds to make it stand out so that the customer reads it. Make those seconds count.

POSTCARDS, DOOR HANGERS AND INVITATIONS

Every day the testing is on. Which color pulls more interest? Is there a better font to use? What message or headline sells best? What method of advertising is best? And so on and so on and on … It's no surprise then to discover that one of the most recent trends has been to use something different from the everyday run-of-the-mill flyer. Sometimes you will find a postcard in amongst the mix. It is true, the thickness, difference in size and personalized information on them does get them noticed, but if that notice is not being converted into calls and sales, then there is something still going wrong for you.

Door hangers are those ads that you find hanging on your door when you come home. It's usually for a pizza delivery service or the like and is quite distinctive in its appearance, thus causing it to definitely be noticed. It is akin to the 'Do not disturb' door hanger notices you see in hotel rooms. The only problem with this kind of delivery is that it costs more, because the deliverer has to do more, and it does not have the same impact with apartment complexes and the like, where you don't have access to the doors. And there are many places these days that don't have door handles as such, but just a keyed entry as a part of the door.

Invitations are very strong in that people love to be invited to something. It makes them feel special and it's something that doesn't happen very often. How many times in a year do you receive a written invitation to an event or happening? Chances are, not that often. And so it is that when prospective customers receive and invitation, they usually at least take the time to read the invitation. However, here's a hand hint, if you have gone to all the trouble of printing and designing an invitation, and then you start the invitation with, 'To the Householder,' you have lost your opportunity. Make the greeting personal. Use a list with the real names of real people. And make the invitation something worth leaving home for. A simple invitation to come down and see what we have to offer won't do it.

DIRECT-MAIL ADVERTISING

More and more, savvy advertisers are discovering that the one method that consistently delivers good results is the direct-mail campaign. This is where you target your ideal customer. This is where you know who your customer is, how much they earn, what they spend their disposable income on and what their problems are. You know them so well in fact, that you are already presenting them with valuable solutions to solve their predicaments, because you alone understand them better than anybody else. And yes it does work.

You contact them at least once a month. You present them with great deals and offers that have huge perceived value for the customer, but costs you little or nothing to supply, and you run a continuity program that is directly linked to all of your promotions.

TESTING FOR SUCCESS

Sadly, this is one of the most neglected aspects of advertising. There are those agencies that will promise you great campaigns that target everyone and everything and will also promise you the best results possible, but they will rarely promise you a testing process that accompanies their campaigns. And this is where novice advertisers (even ones who have been in business for a very long time can get this one wrong), can be dazzled into agreeing with and to everything, just grateful not to have to do anything about advertising. This is a huge and very costly error. If your advertising company cannot provide you with tested campaigns that measure your ROI on each ad, listing, flyer, direct-mail campaign, then they are not worthy of your attention, no matter how small or large your budget is.

Always use some identifying tag, number, response call etcetera to separate out your ads/flyers and then measure the response. For example if you have a café and you are running an ad in the local paper, add a line like 'Free coffee if you bring this ad in.' That way you know exactly what kind of response you have received from the ad, and you are able to calculate how much the cost of each new customer has been to you. If the ad cost you $100, and brought in four new customers, then each new lead has cost you $25. Quite a high cost, possibly, but it's up to you and your café now, to convert that lead into a long term customer, potentially bringing in thousands of dollars over the course of the next ten years or so. But at least you know for sure if the ad worked, and to what extent. It is a measurable entity.

CORPORATE SPONSORS AND STRATEGIC ALLIANCES

Just recently there has been a television advertisement promoting the sale of Ferrero product Kinder Bueno. You buy two Bueno chocolates and you get a movie pass to Hoyts Cinemas all for $5. The retail price for a single bar is about $2.50 so you don't actually save on the chocolate bar price, but you get a free movie ticket. This is a great deal, especially when the cost of a movie ticket can cost up to $20 for an adult.

But here's where the deal gets better, and better and better – for the companies involved. Customers get a free movie ticket, but they will still spend at the snack bar and possibly bring along friends without free tickets who will have to pay. So, for both the cinema company

Hoyts and Ferrero, it's a good deal. They both receive sales. Ferrero doesn't even have to drop the sales price of their item. They simply add the bonus of another company's product. Both parties could split the promotional costs and already everyone wins.

However, one of the terms in the ever present 'Terms and Conditions' states:

Claimants consent to the Promoter using their name, likeness, image and/or voice (including photograph, film and/or recording of the same) in any media for an unlimited period without remuneration for the purpose of promoting this competition (including any outcome), and promoting any products manufactured, distributed and/or supplied by the Promoter.

This means that not only have they been able to amass a huge customer list, but they don't have to pay anyone for their endorsement now or ever. It is quite simply a brilliant arrangement.

Developing strategic alliances within your own business can be a very powerful way of leveraging your advertising budget and expanding your lists and influence, especially if the company or business you are in alliance with, already has good credibility.

If you are running an event as a promotion for the business, for example, you are hosting an engineering expo in your precinct, then have many sponsors promoting the event as well. It's a win-win for all involved.

It sounds like a whole lot of common sense, but it's amazing how many businesses don't think of it, or shy away from it because of a lack of confidence in dealing with other companies. But, it's a great way to develop your own skills in all sorts of ways.

TESTIMONIALS

It's great to hear that a lot of businesses rely on what is called 'word-of-mouth' advertising. It's good to know that there are customers out there doing your promotions for you. Just imagine if you coupled this type of endorsement with other types of advertising. You would be generating a much greater response.

But to talk about testimonials is to discover the real power behind them. We all know that people talk and people listen. If you hear tell of an incident that was not so satisfactory for one of your friends, you will tell people too. In short, the risk businesses run in not implementing exceptional customer service, is huge. But when the talk is good, that's great.

So, what if we took it all one step further. You have all seen the testimonials pages on websites, where there are usually glowing reports about the service or product at hand. And this is always a good thing. It gives you an insight into what people are saying and highlights the experiences they have had. Granted, the bad comments, if there are any, don't get posted. If you visit some online auction sites, there is usually the capacity for comments and messages and so on. It is here where you really get to find out if a product/service is reliable and worth purchasing.

But what if you don't have any testimonials? What do you do? Firstly, don't invent them – that's tacky and always leaves a lingering bad feeling. The best thing to do is to listen to your customers and when they offer some congratulatory words on an aspect of your business, simply say 'Oh thank you. Would you mind if we used that as a testimonial on our website?' Some customers may be shy about it, but most will happily agree, especially if you suggest you write it and have them okay it before it is put up. But don't stop when you have accumulated just a few of them. Granted, you won't post more than about five or six, but if you continue to gather them, you can print them all in a small A5 publication that sits at the front of your office, or use them as an insert to special direct-mail customers. And you can simply call it 'Confirmation' of your excellent service.

CHAPTER EIGHT

SUMMARY

- Hard-copy advertising is an expensive but effective form of advertising. It should be accompanied by a systematic and planned campaign.

- Follow what successful repeat advertisers do in magazines and trade journals and again – make your ad assessable and part of a campaign.

- Newspaper advertising can be costly and ineffective unless it is tagged for ROI and part of a process or campaign. Ad hoc, one off ads do little to promote a business, unless there is an irresistible offer made in the ad.

- Brochures and flyers have little effect if they are distributed along with other 'junk mail'.

- Postcards, door hangers and invitations are stronger forms of advertising if used well and containing good copy and excellent offers. Direct-mail advertising is said to be the strongest, most powerful form of advertising with the best results.

- Corporate sponsorships and strategic alliances are highly efficient forms of leveraging promotional opportunities and extending credibility.

CHAPTER NINE

SAVING YOUR BUSINESS

Without the strength to endure the crisis, one will see the opportunity within. It is within the process of endurance that opportunity reveals itself.

—Chin-Ning Chu

HOPE SPRINGS ETERNAL

The belief that 'hope springs eternal' can be either the salvation or ruination of a business. On the positive side, business owners often believe that 'it'll be alright once ...' What they mean by this is once the market turns, once the weather improves, once the new accountant takes over and once the supplier stock arrives. The trouble with this type of pie in the sky unrealistic hopeful attitude is that there is always another 'once' to follow the last one.

Some businesses can go on like this for years, making greater and greater annual losses, until finally, they have to take an honest look at things and realize they either have to shut the doors forever, or take some major steps to gain control and turn things around. There are individuals who, no matter how big the impending devastation is, will continue to think that all will be well 'once...' and refuse to do anything until the receivers step in over their smiling body and take any further options away from them.

There are those business owners, on the other hand, who have had the courage to take a good solid look at their business situation and summon up the fortitude to do something about it. In other words, they won't go down without a fight.

There was one business owner who was often quoted as saying 'I don't mind looking ugly until I'm rich.' What he meant by this was, he didn't mind having to get down and get his hands dirty while he was building his future and his wealth. If it meant he had to make some unsavory and unpleasant decisions, then so be it. If it meant he had to be unpopular, or considered uncouth, then too bad. He did what he had to do, within the limits of best business practice and moral responsibilities. And now he is living the life that some novices think they should be living as soon as they open the doors to their business.

One of the most important things that successful business owners have in common is their commitment to working long and hard and doing what it takes to get things done. There is not a single one of them who hasn't been through hard times, and many proclaim there were times when they were only a hair's breadth away from the closing the doors.

Jim McCann, founder and CEO of 1-800-FLOWERS.COM, INC., opened his first retail store in 1976 – this is the first sentence of the About Us page for 1800 Flowers. What it doesn't tell you is that when Jim McCann bought the business, he bought it as a going concern, and as such, also bought the debts associated with it. Within a couple of weeks of buying his business, and still in the buzz of it all, he discovered that the company was in serious financial trouble. He hadn't performed enough due diligence when he bought it, and soon found that the tens of thousands of dollars that were owed to creditors, was enough to send him bankrupt before he even began.

He had a discussion with his mother about the situation and the pending bankruptcy that was facing him. His mother told him that in this family, failure is not an option. McCann went away and thought about it. If failure was not an option then what would he have to do to make it succeed.

Well, to make a long story short – there was some free space at the back of the shop – he used it to set up a telephone ordering service, changed the name and is now the world's largest online and offline florist in the US. He did what he had to do to be successful. If failure was not an option even at the most extreme of circumstances, then there had to be other ways to harness the success he was determined to have.

So, before it gets to the bankruptcy stage, ensure you have the systems in place that will require you to assess the progress or decline of your business every month – and be real about it – no 'once the market changes' excuses.

When your business is about to go down the gurgler and there are pending casualties everywhere, staff, suppliers, managers and all the rest, will be sure to come up with a myriad of reasons why none of this was their fault. There will be smoke-screens galore and much ducking and diving. But if failure is not going to be an option for you then seeing the reality of the situation is going to be the only way forward.

Once you have found the honesty and the courage to lift the veil and see things in their true light, you will be able to make real assessments and judgments about how to move forward. There are hundreds of big businesses that have gone through tough times, and they survive. As long as there is cash flow, there is hope. And when you add barter to the mix, there is not only hope, there is the real possibility of turning things around.

SOFTLY SOFTLY DOESN'T WORK

Annette owned a café/restaurant in the middle of town. It was frequented by tourists and locals alike and had been open for some 15 years. However when she bought the business some eight months earlier, Annette hadn't realized that the figures she had been given were bogus, that the rent was exorbitant and that you had to sell a lot of coffee to pay the six staff who worked for her.

In her heart she knew she should let at least two if not three of them go. She knew their wages, along with some other significant hemorrhaging was bleeding the business dry. And yet, week after week as she sat trying to find enough money to pay the wags, she kept justifying to herself why she had to keep them on. Mary had five kids to support and a layabout husband who wouldn't pull his weight. So Annette couldn't fire her. Kathleen was too sweet and would always burst into tears the moment a situation became pressured. So, Annette couldn't fire her either. Lisa just got engaged and was planning a wedding and had an expensive 4x4 she was paying off. So, letting her go was out of the question too. Martha the chef was in the middle of paying for a breeding program for her llamas, so Annette felt she had to keep her on too.

By about month 13 when the banks wouldn't advance her any more loans, when all other options had failed, when there was just no more to give and a whole lot more to pay out, Annette closed the business – and all of them had to look for work.

The irony of the situation is that Annette had to let them all go eventually anyway. They all had to find new employment. If she had had the courage to let two or three of them go earlier, then things may have improved enough to bring them back on board. As it was Annette had to sell her house to pay for the outstanding debts that resulted from her losses.

A common thread from successful business owners, when talking about cutting costs is, be ruthless, be cruel to be kind and cut, cut, cut wherever possible. Leave no stone unturned, no option unexplored. Where there's a way to save a few dollars, take it. Forget about looking pretty. Do what has to be done.

One large corporation once found itself on the brink of closure. The Directors knew they had to make some serious savings. They let the word spread down amongst the rank and file and within 24 hours one of the computer technicians asked to speak with them. He had a suggestion to make. It was embarrassingly simple and could save them huge amounts of money straight away.

'Turn the computers off overnight.' That was it. In fact it was so staggeringly simple that they were taken aback. Then they looked at the costs. Currently, when the hundred or so office workers left at the end of the day, they would leave their computers on, and just flick off the screensavers when they returned the next morning. By turning the computers off every night before they left, they were able to save the company thousands of dollars per year. One simply little action – who would have thought? They also discovered that some workers were getting sloppy and ambivalent in their actions and doing things like sending mail via FedEx instead of regular delivery. There were a myriad of other things they found were draining the money – all things that you can tend to ignore when things are going well. But these things all have an effect and all add up at the end of the month.

This is where barter can be an enormous saving grace. The additional buffer of barter between you and the creditors can mean the difference between dying a slow and painful business death and finding your way out of the mess into a brighter, more organized and successful future.

Where ever possible in times of business turmoil, preserve your cash flow so that essentials can be honored and your reputation preserved. Use barter for anything else that you can. Use it for office stationery, advertising, computers – software and hardware. Only use those suppliers who will accept barter. And take every opportunity that comes your way to preserve and increase cash flow.

HIDING AWAY

Those times in the night when you wake up in a cold sweat with the night terrors and panic, knowing that your life and everything that you hold dear is about to be impacted by your failure, that's when the desire to run and hide is at its worst. And then when you get up in the morning and the terror is still gripping your heart, you begin to act irrationally and many end up doing things that are illegal, immoral or irreparable.

This would be a good time to repeat the words of Winston Churchill: ***Never run away from anything. Never.***

So many times you hear, or know of businesses that have upped and disappeared in the night. One minute they are there trading as usual and the next they're gone – with no-one left to explain about goods, services, creditors except perhaps for the hapless cleaner, who is there on behalf of the landlord anyway.

Desperate people do desperate things and courtrooms are filled with the reasons why desperate acts occur. But when you hide, you cut yourself off from your own strength and power. You cut yourself off from opportunities that may be opening up for you. And you blind yourself to the help and support that is out there for you.

If you have ever been in the position of being involved in a minor car accident – especially if it was your fault, and your car and the other car have to be repaired, you don't hide from the assessor or tell lies to the mechanic or panel beater or spray painter. You don't fail to turn up to the hospital for treatment if your head is bleeding. You don't duck and dive to avoid the doctors. You do whatever you have to do to make things right – mind you, if you haven't bothered to take out insurance, then you may be in a spot of bother, but generally speaking, you know that all of the above contingencies will be covered and that it is just a matter of process before you are able to get out on the road again and enjoy your car. You don't hide away in shame because you had a minor collision. You don't fear facing your friends because you inadvertently had a rear-ender.

It's the same with a failing business. You don't keep hiding until they come to take you away. Some do – but they are often the ones who have been so frightened for so long that they are unable to function like rational adults anymore. Plain and simple truths are lost on them and the way forward, to them, is fraught with more pain, fear, uncertainty, fear, shame, fear and more fear.

If you are in this situation know that it is better to die trying than to die as a coward hiding away from the realities that are facing you. No-one is going to put you down for trying. There will be plenty though, who will have their go, if you don't even try.

PLANNING RECOVERY

Everyone who has ever run a business knows that sometimes it is almost impossible to get to planning and goal orientation when each day seems full of spot fires and emergencies, and staff situations, and customer complications and so on.

Ed, a timber supplier, was unable to hide from his predicament any longer. He had done the usual fear prompted things of not opening mail, avoiding phone calls, only responding to red letters, and ducking and weaving wherever he could to shield himself from the reality of the situation. One morning after another night of terror and cold sweats, he decided that he didn't want to live this way any longer. He simply couldn't do it anymore – he would sooner have walked into an alligator pit than continue on in this way.

He went into the office, told the staff that come hell or high water, he would be unavailable for calls or any other form of interruption, for the whole day. They would just have to carry on without him for that day. That entire day staff looked worriedly at one another and shot many a glance at Ed's closed door. By eight o'clock that evening, Ed stepped out of the office. All the staff had gone, the machines were quiet and the factory was shrouded in darkness, and yet, for Ed at that moment, it was the best thing he had ever seen. He surveyed every inch of the place and was amazed at how far he had already been able to come. He smiled and went home.

Next day he made some announcements to staff – he had put together a recovery plan that catered for all contingencies for the next 12 months. For the first six months, each week had been meticulously planned. For the latter six months, it was more general. He had decided how to approach creditors, and knew that he could arrange payment options for most of them. He knew he had to face his callers and his correspondents. He was planning to do that this morning and set up payment plans for all of the arrears.

He also made one life-changing decision for the business. He would only spend two hours of every day concentrating on problems. The rest of the day would be dedicated to streamlining systems, and engaging in income producing activity, according to the plan he had meticulously mapped out the day before.

Staff were stunned – all at once, they had a boss, someone who knew where they were going and who was now courageous enough to steer them on their new course to success. With Ed's renewed enthusiasm, they found they too were enthused about the business – and surprise, surprise, productivity improved, output increased and there was a general air of hope and anticipation about the business that hadn't been there for a very long time.

Ed had some great ideas about moving his business forward, but had never had the time or the discipline to move them forward before, because he was always too busy putting out the spot fires of the day. He was on a roll. He made the managers manage, the office staff take care of their duties and he was set to spend most of his time working on the business rather than in the business.

Because the banks and creditors could see there was a plan and there was finally communication and intent, they were happy to accommodate Ed in whichever way they could. Finally Ed had engineered a situation where the way forward was not just a pipe dream, but an achievable reality.

Hiding just does not work – it is a reaction based on fear. It is an instinctive way of reacting to fear and the unknown. It is self-preservation at its most basic level. And it rarely achieves anything beyond living in a constant state of fight or flight. There are many who would argue that final stages of growing up occur when one has children and finally when one owns a business. When you *have* to be responsible, alert, active, impassioned and determined in the face of great odds, then there are very few who can stand alongside you. And this is when success is sweetest.

THE RECOVERY PLAN

Having your ideas for recovery in your head and knowing where you're aiming to be in 12 months' time is a good thing. If it's not on paper though, you could be setting yourself up for more failure and dismal times. If you have been putting it off because words 'are not your thing' then go online and source the templates that are available. There are many options that you can choose from that will give you access to forms, templates, suggestions, outlines and references. But, have a plan you must. At least you will have something tangible to hand to bankers and creditors that lets them know, that you have planned a recovery and that things are organized and under control.

A good recovery plan should give detailed attention to the following factors:

- Introduction.
- Description and reasons for decline.
- Description of the restructure (including management).
- Amended marketing strategies.
- Product/service review.
- Financial revlew.
- Financial recovery
- Extra options.
- Appendix.

Introduction

The introduction to your recovery plan should provide all the contact details, the basic structure of the business or company as it currently exists, list the directors, major investors and any other defining features of the business.

The second section of the introduction will give a carefully con-
structed outline (1–2 paragraphs only) of the recovery strategies
expecting to be implemented.

Description and reasons for decline

This section really should be quite succinct and objective. This is not
intended to be the repository for vilification or the venting of the spleen.
Save that for your diary or blog. This section should give objective
statements only. For example: 'The global credit crunch resulted in the
loss of 57 clients, who were forced into foreclosure and subsequent
bankruptcy. This meant that accounts to the value of $67,000 were
not able to be honored, and have been tabled as a loss. There are no
foreseeable avenues of recovering these funds.'

Statements such as 'My loser brother-in-law was too busy wasting
time and money to keep a professional eye on the books', is not the
type of thing to write here, primarily because this recovery plan can
and should be viewed by those who are going to be able to help you to
recover. This is not the time for personal wailing and horsewhipping.

You may also state some basic methodologies you have employed
to prevent these factors from affecting your business again: e.g.
future invoices will include strict 30 day terms only, with deposits and
guarantees required for amounts over $3,000.

Descriptions of the restructure – including management

Within this section there should be subsections that mention each part
of your business. If you are an office equipment supplier, then mention
should be made of your staffing; production; processes; sales and
marketing; wastage; accounting and projections.

You should also list the major contributors to the turn around. For
example, if your office equipment business has had recurring problems
that have impacted on your profitability, then this is the time to mention,
loud and clear, the methods you intend to employ to eradicate those

limitations. If you have had a faulty on/off switch that has resulted in many returns and so on, and you have neglected to fix that problem, then do the responsible thing and demonstrate how you plan to repair the machines and adjust the design fault so that future machines won't be susceptible to the same limitations and rejections. It should be as detailed as that. It should include projections and aspirations and talk about your renewed vigor and strength in the market.

Wherever possible, a positive angle regarding each and every major problem, should be adopted. No-one wants to take a chance on someone who is wallowing in their misery and doesn't have the strength to stand up and not only accept responsibility but accountability as well. Even Barack Obama had the strength of character to say to the American people, and the world, 'The buck stops here.' And so it does with every business owner. When it's tough and bad and ugly, take control. Don't hide away and cringe. Stand up. Be accountable and move on. Everyone loves a success story that has been borne of disaster and near ruination – no-one loves a loser who just walked away without giving it their best shot.

Amended marketing strategies

Right, so you've got your finances back in order. You've talked about your recovery strategies and your implementation policies. You've impressed all and sundry with your come-back routine and you've thrown open the doors to welcome the adoring throngs ready to throw checks at you. But wait – there is no-one. That was not how the plan was meant to operate. There were meant to be hordes. You had planned on hordes. Great ads, lots of posters, many invitations and new staff uniforms, and still no hordes. Just what does it take to get the hordes?

Well, as dull as it may seem, if you haven't adjusted and rethought your marketing approach, then there will be little or no change to the responses you receive. Guess it doesn't take rocket science to work that one out.

It is absolutely, positively, incredibly important that in your recovery plan you address the all-important subject of Advertising and Marketing. This part of your business is most often responsible for the amount of custom you receive. It is responsible for your perceived standing in the market and it is responsible for your image amongst your customers.

If cash flow is a problem for your business then this is the number one way to get back on track without wasting your precious cash. Using barter for revamping and overhauling your advertising and marketing is the intelligent way to advertise your new look business. It's the best way to get to be known 'out there' for your re-launch. And the news gets even better. Absolutely every form of advertising and marketing is generally offered on barter.

Your television and radio ads, that once would have sucked up a huge amount of capital, can now be aired without the headache of wondering where the costs are going to come from. Your radio ads can be more frequent, because your budget is less constrained and the printing costs for your mail outs, flyers, stationery and postcards, can all be paid for using barter.

And it gets even better still. Those internet hosting and designing services that would have been out of your reach, are now completely workable for you because of barter.

You can re-vamp your website, re-design your approach, pay for hosting and maintenance and not have to pay a cent. You can hire a writer, a graphic designer, a web designer and a host of others required for the professional look, and never have to dispense with your precious cash reserves. This is extremely important when you are trying to convince bankers, creditors, loan managers and the like, of your ability to get things back on track.

If they can see you have a coordinated and costed a plan that is going to bring in results – i.e. more paying customers, then they will have few, if any objections to your new look operation.

Product/service review

When the winds of disaster have ripped through your business, there is no better time for a great big clean up. This is the best opportunity you will legitimately have for doing the most thorough clean up possible. This is where you will be able to fire those hangers on that have been dragging you down. This is where you get rid of those systems that have not been serving you well. This is where you move location, if you have to, to another place that will be better for your bottom line. This is where you shake up the design and manufacturing departments and tell them once and for all to fix the problems you have been having with the product or move on. This is where those advertisers who have not been producing measurable results can be given the flick.

You've heard the saying 'A new broom sweeps clean' but there is no cleaner sweep than that of the business owner on a mission – and what better mission can there possibly be than that of saving your business from ruination?

Here too barter can be of real use. If there are service providers and product designers who are available on barter, use them. If there are supporting goods and services that can be accessed on barter, use them too.

It will be another indication to your bankers and creditors that you are serious about the turnaround. It will show them in black and white, that the renewed you is possible and probable and very achievable. They won't have to be relying on if's and maybe's when you have presented them with the cold facts of what is.

This is also a golden opportunity for you to drag out of the dusty cupboard, that prototype you have been wanting to develop but have never had the time. It is just the time to re-invent your product with the extra bells and whistles that you know will catapult it into the next level of whizz bang genius. There are hundreds of companies that have come back from the brink with the introduction of a new or amended product that has proved much more successful than the original. Your business can be one of them.

However, a word of warning – make sure the product is market ready and tested for launching into the market. A half-baked 'almost' product will not do. You will simply be setting your business up for another bruising. And that's the last thing you need. If your new product has been researched, tested, designed according to market demand, then go for it. Heard of the Apple iPad?

Financial review

No, this isn't the newspaper we are talking about. It's the review of the financial status of your business. This is where the brave and the bold really are separated from those who are only playing at owning a business. Once you have summoned up the courage to open all the red letters and make a comprehensive list of your incomings, outgoings and creditors' bills, then you will have a realistic picture of how deep your pit of despair is.

Sometimes it can be a relief just to see it all laid out in black and white – no judgments, no accusations or recriminations, just numbers on a page. From here the only way out is up. From here you are able to look at each section of your finances and make adjustments.

We have already talked about being ruthless in your cost-cutting, staff shedding and renewal of business systems and product. This is no place to lose heart. You have done all the really hard bits. This is just one more task on the way to the sheer and utter bliss that will come to you when you realize that you are really and truly on the road to recovery.

Where possible, call your creditors and arrange a payment plan. Even the taxation office will allow you to re-pay according to a pre-arranged plan and they won't kill you if you are able to stick to it. They will even give you extensions and financial advice and support if you need it. Everyone knows you can't get blood out of a stone and as long as you are able to keep your doors open and bring in some cash flow, they will usually understand. Receiving small regular payments is better than receiving nothing at all – or worse still finding that a business has disappeared in the night with no recourse to recompense.

Make a list of the payment plans you have instituted and map out their viability – i.e. state the income sources the payments will be drawn from. And then write up a 12 month forecast with a five-year overview. It would be very surprising to have someone reject a business owner who was so thorough in his/her approach and so determined to make it work.

Financial recovery

Your financial recovery isn't just about notations on paper or spreadsheets. It is about a big-picture approach that takes into account every aspect of your finances. It is about the petty cash. It is about the budgets. It is about the incomings and outgoings and most especially about the P&L statements. If you need to hire an accountant or business advisor or financial advisor to help you in this regard then do it – using barter, and then add their name to your recovery plan so that your creditors are able to see that you have used the advice of financial experts to help you out.

The other sections of the recovery plan are fairly self-explanatory and less vital than those cited above. However add them as you choose and put in the information that you feel would be relevant to your cause.

CHAPTER NINE

SUMMARY

- If there is the faintest bit of life left in your business, then there is the hope of saving it.

- Be ruthless in your cost cutting and forget about other people's feelings and situations – you can commiserate with each other on the unemployment line.

- Hiding from the problems won't help you – it will make things worse.

- Put together an intelligent, viable and achievable Recovery Plan that encompasses all aspects of your business.

- Present your recovery plan to bankers, creditors, loan managers and the like to demonstrate the determination and organization of your recovery.

- No-one likes a loser who gave up without a fight.

CHAPTER TEN

THE BUSINESS OF BARTER

When you confront a problem you begin to solve it
—Rudy Giuliani

Without the strength to endure the crisis, one will see the opportunity within. It is within the process of endurance that opportunity reveals itself.
—Chin-Ning Chu

There are those business owners who are able to turn a profit no matter what the circumstances. We say that they have 'The Midas Touch' or everything they touch turns to gold. We call them lucky, or say that someone must be looking after them. We give them all sorts of superhuman attributes and we look at them with awe and wonder. And then we start to make excuses for why our own businesses and situations are failing.

There are no magic bullets, no free rides, no insider information for them alone, no access to hidden files or fortunes – it all comes down to one basic tenet – the harder you work the luckier you are. And before we go on, let us qualify what it means to say 'hard work'. For some the interpretation is nothing short of moving one pile of boulders from one place to another, all the while exerting huge amounts of energy and pressure and never being released from it. And in the history of events that is how most of us have been educated and raised. We think that life is meant to be tough, that nothing good came from nothing down. But hard work, can also mean consistent effort. Yes there are tales of those who have been very successful from just a few hours a week of consistent effort, usually internet business owners, but it is possible.

In essence it's the working consistently and doggedly that is the secret – and making use of good information that is going to improve your business regularly. You know that your books have to be in order. You know that your suppliers and your producers have to provide you will quality pieces that are worth what you pay for them. You know that you are getting the best deals possible with all of those people you deal with. You know that your team has to be onside. You know that you are the leader and basically they will all do as you do. You know too that the pressure on the cash dollar is phenomenal and not a day goes by without a new pressure being found for it. The latest equipment costs more. The updates cost more. Staff pay rates are going up. Repayment rates are on the rise. Utilities cost more than ever and that's just the tip of the iceberg. Having a huge relief from those pressures in the form of Barter is a great advantage to any business owner. Knowing how to use that advantage has been outlined in detail above.

So just what are the initial steps involved in acquiring and setting up your exciting new business? What is involved and what is the best way you can use barter to make this step more successful than simply setting up a business using cash and credit alone?

BARTER AND THE INTERNET

Some businesses pay tens of thousands of cash dollars just to set up a website for their businesses. Often they know little about the process, or simply don't have the time to be bothered with all the detail. And the thing about having to pay for hosting is that it is an ongoing cost – just like line rental for your telephones, only this line rental can be a very significant amount. What could you do if you didn't have to spend cash on this continuing expense? And what about all the updates that have to me made to keep your business abreast with all that is happening in your industry? That's not cheap either. Wouldn't you like to keep the cash that would normally be involved in paying someone to keep your site updated? And then there's the graphic designer, the copywriter, the video producer. The list is constant and demanding. And all of them need paying.

Daunting yes – especially if cash payment is the only alternative that you have. But all of these services can be paid for with barter. You can have a very sophisticated website and associated services all for no cash down. Having them all available as a regular payment that doesn't involve the use of cash, is of great benefit to your business. And it can open up other avenues for your cash flow, so your business isn't always struggling, but is able to grow and keep pace with others in your industry. You would be crazy to let an opportunity like this get away. It is possible to grow your business online without using cash flow.

BARTER AND REAL ESTATE

If your business is able to purchase real estate then having a significant percentage, or all of it available on barter, means that tens of thousands of cash dollars can be preserved. There are realtors who will accept their fee with barter dollars. There are scores of contractors who will renovate and repair or update the real estate you have purchased, without the use of cash. They are happy to accept barter dollars as their payment.

If you are a developer, then purchasing, renovating and flipping are all possible using barter. There can be quite a regular routine to it all once you use barter, that will preserve your cash dollar and grow your wealth simultaneously.

Using a component of barter for your real estate purchases makes great sense. Using barter for as much as you can for your realty needs makes much more sense. Even in prosperous times, holding on to your cash reserves, is the best way to grow your wealth.

BARTER AND EVERYDAY BUSINESS EXPENSES

We know that small to medium businesses in the country are the nation's biggest employers. And we know that around 80% of small businesses fail in the first five years. The odds are bad to begin with but don't get any better with the continual onslaught of outgoing expenses that need to be paid. This is the number one reason so many thousands of businesses fail – they simply don't have the cash flow needed to sustain the business until it is established.

That is why the use of barter in preserving cash flow is such a big deal in keeping the business open in the early days and helping it to thrive later on. Pay your refurbishment costs with barter. Buy your office equipment with barter. Have your communications systems and internet paid for with barter. Use barter for staff incentives and rewards. Pay suppliers with barter dollars. Pay for your crucial advertising and marketing costs with barter. It all adds up to a huge advantage over those who don't know of barter or who are reticent to use it. And there is even better news. In times of economic downturn, barter use thrives even more. Business owners are keener than ever to hold on to their cash reserves and so the number of barter outlets also increases. It is the ultimate win-win situation. Why would any business be without it?

BARTER AND LIFESTYLE

Working 24/7, saving, scrimping, getting things up and running, burning the candle at both ends – are all phrases that are used repeatedly to describe the difficulties in setting up and maintaining a business. You want some reward for all of your hard work don't you? Of course you do – and here's where many a business owner falls. They think that they should be rewarded, and they should, so they go out and get the best of everything they can't afford, try to write it off against the business and then realize there is nothing left to run the business with. The cash reserves have gone, the incoming cash is slow to arrive and bingo, their problems are only just starting. They begin riding the carousel that never stops, never lets them off and never lets them change direction.

With the use of barter, you can have your business, grow your business and have rewards as well. Barter will pay for the fancy resorts, restaurants, adventure tours and five-star hotels – without paying cash. You and your family will be able to enjoy the real fruits of your labour and you will be able to wine and dine whomever you choose. It is the perfect solution to the lifestyle / workplace dilemma.

CONCLUSION

People who ask confidently get more than those who are hesitant and uncertain. When you've figured out what you want to ask for, do it with certainty, boldness and confidence.

—Jack Canfield

BEATING SELF DEFEAT

It is so easy to be overwhelmed by negativity. It is everywhere, pervades every little aspect of our lives and threatens with more destruction at every turn. There are the wars, the natural disasters, man killing man, brother fighting brother, turmoil, distrust, anger, shame, fear, desperation. We turn on the radio – and we are updated every 15 minutes with the latest horror. We turn on the television at the end of the day and there it is again – more disaster, fear and threats. We talk to our neighbors and it's on our own lips and theirs. Our families are swathed in it. We are all influenced by it and we are all affected by it.

How is it possible then to throw all of that aside and be positive? Is it really something we can do? When Mother Teresa first started working in the streets of India helping the destitute and impoverished, she was stoned for her efforts. She was spat upon, derided and cursed. Her life was in constant danger. How is it possible that she was able to rise above all of that to achieve the wonderful things that she did? She was once asked to join a walk against war – she said she would never consider that. She also said however, that if she were asked to walk for peace, she would be there in an instant. For her, life was about being positive always. It was about looking in the face of defeat a thousand times a day and doing it anyway.

Taken from a famous poem. *Do It Anyway*, written by Mother Teresa herself, she states:

What you spend years building,
someone could destroy overnight;
Build anyway.

If you find serenity and happiness,
they may be jealous;
Be happy anyway.

The good you do today, people will
forget tomorrow,
Do good anyway.

These powerful words remind us that focussing on the positive is the result of an attitude. It's what happens when you choose to be on the bright side. It's the side you choose whenever you have to make a decision. It's not about being a deluded Mary Poppins and glossing over problems – it is about being intelligent, open to alternatives and always seeing the positive ramifications of your actions. What you concentrate on is what you become – if you embrace fear, negativity, derision, blame, aggression, then those are the things that will be apparent in your life – in all aspects of it. If you take those same emotions and turn them around then you will see things such as courage, optimism, praise, honour and support as the guiding factors in your life. Which would you prefer?

There is the story told of some survivors of the Auschwitz concentration camps of WWII. They were asked how it was that, for some of them, after years of suffering the most horrendous and unspeakable tortures, they didn't just give up and die. Why had they hung on so tenaciously to life when countless others had been slaughtered and were dying around them? Many of them had the same kind of reply. They had had love and happiness in their childhoods and knew that this kind of atrocity couldn't go on forever. They knew that it would all have to end sometime and that they would be able to somewhere, somehow find happiness again.

In amidst all of that sheer horror they were able to look to the positive and wait for the good to come out of it all. Some would argue that it never did – others would argue that only good came of it.

So, when you're faced with the pain, and drudgery and problems and staff bickering and books that don't tally, and unwanted creditors calling at all hours – stop, smell the roses, find a motivational inspirational mentor and do it anyway. Succeed anyway. Love anyway. Live anyway. Enjoy anyway. That's what Zorba did!

> *I've been to the mountaintop. And I've looked over.*
> *And I've seen the promised land.*
>
> —Martin Luther King

THE VIEW FROM THE MOUNTAINTOP

There have been endless analogies between running a business and running a race, or being a competitor, or climbing a mountain, or driving a car or whatever comparison you choose, it has probably been used, and with good reason. Running a successful business is a marathon with few perks, breaks, redeeming features and always there is more to be done. But these drawbacks don't compare with the freedom of standing at the top of your game, the top of the mountain, and looking around and knowing that you did it – you made it happen. Your success is well-deserved. For some the view from the top is so wonderful and awe-inspiring that they are brought to tears with the sheer joy of it all.

Some of us however, wouldn't know a mountain top if we fell off it. Some of us are so accustomed to the struggle and the toil and the sheer hard yards, that even when the mountain top is under our feet, we don't believe and just start to moan on about something else.

Isn't one of the major reasons for starting your own business, the freedom that it brings you – the release from the yoke of someone else's dream? Isn't it the allowing of the passion within your own heart? Isn't it the satisfaction of seeing the fruits of you labor? Isn't it all because of your own desires? If it isn't, then why are you bothering at all.

Taking time to see the wonder and beauty of what you have achieved is a strong factor in keeping you motivated to attempt the next challenge and the one after that and the one after that – it's the stuff of life – moving forward, making it happen, changing the present into a better future. It's the passion that drives mankind forward into the continual creation of new life. What a waste to be presented with all that and still find something to complain about!

The view is magnificent. It is whatever you want it to be. It is panoramic, all-inclusive and fabulous to boot. You made it. You did it. You have it. You deserve it. You took the trouble to figure it all out and now the reward is yours. Enjoy it. But enjoy it even more with barter – be smart. Make it work for you.

Tough times, good times, happy times, beleaguered times – all times are good with the use of barter. You can barter your way out of almost any situation. It has been done many times and will continue to be done by many savvy business owners and operators. The best time is now.

OTHER TITLES IN

THE SECRET CURRENCY
SERIES BY VERNE GARDINER

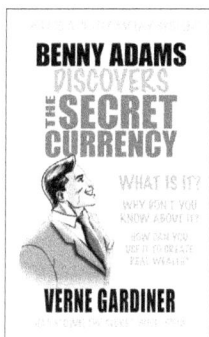

BENNY ADAMS DISCOVERS THE SECRET CURRENCY is the journey of a successful sports agent who has a life of luxury. Becoming a victim of the credit crunch, Benny is financially wiped out, his integrity destroyed and his family left in despair. Turning to an old school chum Tony Corletti, Benny finds a fresh start learning key lessons along the way on how to turn it all around. The journey of Benny is familiar to so many people right now and by learning key strategies from his journey you too can rebuild your life or prevent it from crashing around you.

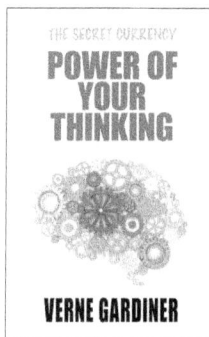

THE POWER OF YOUR THINKING is a personal development tool that will open your eyes to the ways of success. What you thought you knew about yourself and how you operate in a professional environment will be challenged as you learn new skills and build greater business resilience. Now more than ever is the time to look at what other people are doing to grow their business. You can use their secrets and the *Power of Your Thinking* will show you how.

Think outside the square and dare to challenge the norm. By becoming part of the endless evolution of The Secret Currency series you can gain exclusive access to some of the most vital tips for achieving a prosperous work/life. To find out more register at: **www.thesecretcurrency.co**

www.ingramcontent.com/pod-product-compliance
Lightning Source LLC
LaVergne TN
LVHW021457080426
835509LV00018B/2312